GCSE RE for you

Judaism
with Jewish moral issues

GCSE RE for you

Judaism
with Jewish moral issues

INA TAYLOR

Published in 2001 by:
Nelson Thornes Ltd
Delta Place
27 Bath Road
CHELTENHAM
GL53 7TH
United Kingdom

01 02 03 04 05 / 10 9 8 7 6 5 4 3 2 1

A catalogue record for this book is available from the British Library

ISBN 0-7487-5685-X

Illustrations by Jane Taylor and Oxford Designers & Illustrators
Page make-up by Pentacor

Printed and bound in China by Midas

Contents

Topic 1

Brief history and symbols

The Star of David is the best-known symbol of Judaism. It is sometimes called Magen David in Hebrew, meaning 'shield of David'. It is thought that King David may have had this device on his shield when he led his people into battle. Today the Star of David is in the centre of the Israeli flag. The stripes on either side remind Jews of the tallit (see page 27).

 **What is ...?**

A six-pointed star is called the **Star of David**. This is a modern symbol of Judaism and the state of Israel.

 **What is ...?**

A seven-branched candlestick is called a **menorah** and reminds Jews of the candlestick in their original Temple in Jerusalem. The menorah is one of the oldest symbols of Judaism.

The Jews have been known by various other names in their history: Hebrews after the language they spoke, and Israelites, a name they gave to the land they settled. Their history goes back 4,000 years to Abraham, who is regarded as the father of the Jewish race. He was born in the country that is now called Iraq. Jews believe God made the first agreement, or covenant, with Abraham which marked the Jews out as God's chosen race (see page 22). Abraham was told to walk his tribe 1,400 miles to a new country, now called Israel. God promised him: *'I will give you many descendants, and they will become a great nation'* (Genesis 12:2). Jews believe they are all descendants of Abraham, so he is known as a patriarch, or the founding father of their religion.

Other Jews throughout history who have received messages from God are called prophets. The greatest Jewish prophet was Abraham's descendant, Moses. With God's help, Moses led the Jews from slavery in Egypt back to Israel and he was personally given the rules of life (the Torah) by God. Moses' descendant, David, went on to create one nation out of the Jewish tribes. King David, as he became, holds an important place in Jewish history and is remembered in the Jewish symbol, the Star of David.

King David established Jerusalem as the capital of the new land and at its heart was the Temple, the centre for the worship of the one God. This building was considered holy because it housed the two original tablets of stone that God gave to Moses. The laws were written on these tablets.

In the Temple a seven-branched oil lamp, called the menorah, burned continually as a sign of the everlasting presence of God. The menorah has become one of the important symbols of Judaism.

The Temple was attacked and destroyed twice. The second destruction by the Romans in 70 CE was so severe that no attempt was made to rebuild it. Today only one piece of the wall of the original Temple remains; it is called the Western Wall and is the holiest site in Judaism. Jewish settlement in Israel has never been trouble-free. There have been many invasions, occupations and disputes over land, despite the country being given international recognition as the Jewish homeland in 1948. Battles continue into the 21st century.

Activity

- Look on the internet for information and pictures of the Western Wall.
- Can you discover who built the First and Second Temples?

This symbol of Judaism is called a menorah. It is based on the candlestick that stood in the original Temple. Its seven branches are said to remind Jews of the seven days of creation and of the tree of life.

Questions

1 Name two symbols of Judaism and explain their meaning.
2 Why is each of these people important in Jewish history?
  - Abraham
  - Moses
  - David
3 What was the Temple and why was it important to Jews?

Topic 2

Types of Judaism

Numerically the Jews form one of the smallest of the six world religions. Today there are around 17 million Jews in the world, with the largest number living in America. Israel, the Jewish homeland, has a population of around 5.5 million. In Britain there are 280,000 Jews living mainly in cities like London, Manchester and Leeds. Being Jewish doesn't stop a person also being Italian or Russian. A person is Jewish because they were born Jewish. Some Jews believe that Judaism can only be inherited from your mother, while others say you are Jewish if one of your parents was Jewish. It is possible to convert to Judaism, although this is uncommon.

It is very easy to label a person as Jewish and to assume that all Jews believe the same things and practise the same traditions. They don't. In fact there are some Jews who hold no religious beliefs and do not keep any Jewish rituals. They are Jewish because they were born Jewish. These people are known as secular Jews. As in all religions there is a wide range of religious beliefs and practices, from people who call themselves Jewish but only celebrate the festivals, to those for whom religious observance is an essential part of daily life.

The Orthodox Jews

Jews who try to follow the rules in the scriptures as strictly as possible are known as Orthodox Jews. Even within this large group there are many branches of Judaism, with names like the Hasidic movement, Conservative Judaism and the Lubavitz organisation. Some, but not all, Orthodox Jews wear a style of clothing that has remained unchanged since the 19th century. Orthodox Jews believe that God gave people rules about how they should live their lives. These rules were for all people for all time and must be obeyed. Changing them would be disobeying God. Orthodox Jews believe that men and women were given different roles in life at the time of Creation. These differences should remain. Men have an important part to play in synagogue worship, and women in leading worship in the home. Neither sex is regarded as inferior or superior to the other; they are simply different.

The Reform Jews

There are other groups of Jews who believe that Judaism is a living religion which should move with the times. Because this involves reforming the old way of doing things, it is often known as Reform Judaism. In fact, Reform Judaism is only one branch of this modern movement, and there are others like Liberal Judaism and Progressive Judaism. For ease in using this book, all these movements will be called Reform Judaism.

What is ...?

Orthodox Jews believe they should live their lives as close to the rules laid down in the Torah as possible.

What is ...?

Followers of **Reform Judaism** believe the Jewish religion should move with the times.

The Jewish man in the centre is a member of an Orthodox community. He wears traditional clothing with long side-locks of hair. The people on the left are Reform Jews who lead a modern lifestyle. All are Jewish.

Outwardly a Reform Jew is indistinguishable from everyone else, wearing fashionable clothes and living a modern lifestyle. Nevertheless Reform Jews hold similar beliefs about God to those of Orthodox Jews, although they may not use so much ritual in their worship. Reform Jews believe that men and women have equal roles in society today which should be reflected in their worship. In a Reform synagogue, men and women sit together and a woman can wear a tallit if she wishes. It is not uncommon to see a woman rabbi or chazan. Because they take an equal part in synagogue worship, women can stand in the bimah and read from the scrolls. A girl's coming-of-age ceremony is exactly the same as a boy's.

Reform Jews believe that religion should move with the times, so they do not attempt to carry out the words of the Torah literally. On Shabbat a Reform Jewish family will enjoy the Friday meal together, but they may not keep the other Shabbat rules as strictly. They say that the 39 types of work forbidden for Jews in the desert 3,000 years ago no longer make sense today. So they may drive to the synagogue rather than walk, and perhaps go shopping on Saturday afternoon rather than spend the day quietly at home with the whole family. Reform Jews may well keep kosher when eating at home but may eat in a non-kosher restaurant or with non-Jewish friends. Others might compromise by following a vegetarian diet when eating out. Reform Jews argue that it is not realistic to follow the Torah rules to the letter. These rules were given to the Jewish race a long time ago to help them organise themselves into a society at that time.

Questions

1 What makes a person Jewish?
2 List three differences in the ways Orthodox Jews and Reform Jews conduct their lives.
3 What reasons do Reform Jews give for the way they interpret the Torah? What would an Orthodox Jew say to this?

Holy places

The Western Wall is an open-air synagogue. The women in the picture are pushing folds of paper with prayers into the cracks between the stones.

 What is ...?

The **Western Wall** is the most sacred place in Judaism. It is the last remaining part of the original Temple in Jerusalem.

Western Wall

Many Jews like to go to places that have played an important part in their religious history, but pilgrimage is not a religious obligation in Judaism. Visiting some of the places where momentous events happened in the past can help a Jew feel closer to God. Jews believe that God has intervened many times in their history to help the Jewish people, and Israel has a large number of sacred sites where events like this took place, as well as tombs of great rabbis and prophets. It is, however, Jerusalem, the holy city, that has been the focal point of worship throughout history. Every year Jews who sit around the table to celebrate the festival of Pesach raise their wineglasses to the traditional toast: 'Next year in Jerusalem!' They face in the direction of Jerusalem for their daily prayers.

Jerusalem is important to Jews because it was founded by King David and because it is the site of the Temple. Although the Temple was destroyed twice and only a small section of its wall remains now, it is still the focus of Jewish worship. Many Jews like to visit the Western Wall to pray because for them this is the holiest place on earth. Some families travel to Israel to celebrate their son's Bar Mitzvah at the Wall, and some couples who marry in Jerusalem go to the Wall for prayers after their wedding ceremony. Prayers are said at the Western Wall every day and several of the major festivals are celebrated there. Today it is an open-air synagogue with a section for male worshippers and a separate one for female worshippers.

Masada

Another place that Jews visit is Masada. Here are the remains of an ancient hilltop fort overlooking the Dead Sea. In 70 CE, the same year that the Romans conquered Jerusalem and destroyed the Temple, they also swept through the country killing all Jews who resisted. One group of Jews, determined not to give in to the might of Rome, fled to this hilltop retreat. For three years they held out until finally the Romans began breaching the walls. A total of 960 Jews committed suicide rather than surrender to the enemy. Jewish visitors to Masada today are inspired by their ancestors' bravery. This place has come to symbolise Jewish determination that their country must remain free, summed up by the famous words, 'Masada will not fall again'.

Masada is an ancient hill fort near the Dead Sea. For Jews it is a symbol of freedom.

To many Jews the ancient hill fort of Masada is also a symbol of nationalism.

Yad Vashem

A more recent holy place that Jews visit for prayer and quiet contemplation is the Holocaust memorial park near Jerusalem, called Yad Vashem. It was established in 1953 as a lasting memorial to the 6 million Jews who were killed by the Nazis in the Second World War. Most have no grave. They are remembered through sculptures and exhibits. Visitors to Yad Vashem find it a powerful and moving experience. Some like to light a candle in memory of the dead. (There is more information about Yad Vashem on page 85.)

? Questions

1 Name three places that have a special religious significance for Jews.
2 What sort of religious actions might a Jew perform at the Western Wall?
3 Why is Jerusalem such an important place for Jews?
4 'If pilgrimage doesn't matter to Jews, why do they go to these places?' How would you answer that question?

Do you understand...
Judaism?

Task 1

1 This statue is outside the Israeli parliament in Jerusalem. What does it represent?
2 What is the other very well-known symbol of Judaism? Where does it get its name?

Task 2

1 What was the Temple and why was it important to Jews?
2 a What might a Jewish person who visits this place do today?
  b What ceremonies might take place here?
3 'Places where things happened in the past are no help to people today.' What do you think? Give reasons for your answer, showing that you have considered more than one point of view.

This is the last remaining piece of the Temple.

Task 3

Divide a page in your notebook in half lengthwise. Head one column '**Orthodox Judaism**' and the other '**Reform Judaism**'. List as many differences as you can discover between these two major divisions in Judaism. You may need to look further on in the book for information.

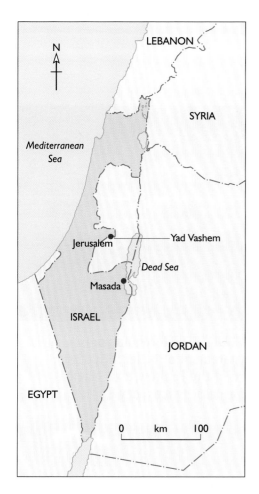

Task 4

Why are Jerusalem, Yad Vashem and Masada all important sacred sites for Jews?

Task 5

How many of these words can you define?
- Menorah
- the Temple
- patriarch
- Star of David
- Orthodox Judaism
- Masada
- Yad Vashem

Quick revision

- The menorah and the Star of David are two symbols of Judaism.
- The Temple was finally destroyed by the Romans in 70 CE.
- Reform Judaism believes the religion should move with the times.
- Judaism is inherited from the mother.
- Orthodox Judaism follows the Torah as closely as possible.

Topic 1

Concepts of God

Jews believe that God is the creator of everything in the world. Our encounter with things in nature is like an encounter with God.

What is ...?

The **Shema** is the most important Jewish prayer. It is also the basic statement of belief in Judaism.

'Hear O Israel, the Lord our God is one God.' (Deuteronomy 6:4) This is the Shema, the most important statement of belief in Judaism. The name comes from the opening word of the Hebrew text, 'shema', meaning 'hear'. A Jew states this belief at least twice a day in their morning and evening prayer.

Unity of God

The Shema sums up the Jews' basic belief in the existence of one God that cannot be divided into parts like a father and a son. God is without gender, although for convenience God is usually referred to as 'he'. Jews believe that God is unique, never born or created and never dying. To Jews God is eternal. Everything in existence is under God's control. Many Jewish prayers open with the words, 'Blessed art Thou, O Lord our God, King of the Universe'.

God the creator and sustainer of life

The first words in the Torah, the Jewish scriptures, are:
'In the beginning, when God created the universe, the earth was formless and desolate.' (Genesis 1:1)

Jews believe that God created the heavens and the earth out of nothing. They also believe that creation was not a one-off event millions of years ago. It continues every new day as plants and animals grow and the seasons change. Humans have the chance to share in God's work of creation by having children.

Activity

Learn the first line of the Shema so that you can write it from memory. This is a favourite exam question!

Jews believe God sustains, or looks after, the universe he created. The life force is poured into it continually, and essential things for existence, like food, water and air, are provided by God. Everything depends on God for its existence. Jews also believe that God does intervene in the world to change the course of events. They look back to various times in their history when God has intervened to save them.

God as law-giver and judge

Jews believe that God has shown them the correct way to lead their lives. Rules, called mitzvot in Hebrew, were given to the prophet Moses on Mount Sinai in the form of the Torah. Jews should obey these rules. God has given them free-will to choose whether they do or not. When a person dies they will be judged on how they used their free-will. Those who have kept God's rules will be rewarded by closeness to God. Those who have disobeyed the rules will be punished. However, Jews believe God is merciful and will forgive people who are genuinely sorry for their wrongs and have tried to make amends.

The Messianic Age

It is believed that God will save the world at some time in the future. A spiritual leader, called the Messiah, will arrive on earth to lead the Jews into a time of peace for all living creatures.

Jews believe that at some time in the future there will be a God-given period of peace on the planet. They call this the **Messianic Age**.

This is a detail from the Messianic window in a London synagogue. It shows the idea of peace that is described in the book of Isaiah 11:6–8:

'Wolves and sheep will live together in peace,
and leopards will lie down with young goats...
Calves and lion cubs will feed together,
and little children will take care of them.
Cows and bears will eat together,
and their calves and cubs will lie down in peace.
Lions will eat straw as cattle do.'

Can you identify some of these features in the window?
There is also another traditional symbol of peace in the window.

Questions

1 What is the Shema?
2 Why is the Shema the most important prayer in Judaism?
3 What do Jews mean when they say God is eternal?
4 What is meant by the Messianic Age?
5 'Creation wasn't something that happened millions of years ago.' Why would a Jew say that?

Topic 2

The Torah

This window shows an imaginary scene of the ark of the covenant which contained the two tablets of stone in the Temple.

Orthodox Jews believe that God revealed to Moses exactly how the Jews should lead their lives. On Mount Sinai Moses received the laws which have been written down in five books called the Torah.

'If you obey the commands of the Lord your God, which I give you today, if you love him, obey him, and keep all his laws, then you will prosper and become a nation of many people. The Lord your God will bless you in the land that you are about to occupy. But if you disobey and refuse to listen, and are led away to worship other gods, you will be destroyed – I warn you here and now.

(Deuteronomy 30:16–18)

 Activity

Learn the names of the five books of the Torah so that you can recite them from memory:
- Genesis
- Exodus
- Leviticus
- Numbers
- Deuteronomy.

The Ten Commandments appear in Hebrew above the ark. The name of God has been removed from this picture because Orthodox Jews think it is disrespectful to write such a sacred word on paper that might be destroyed. The name of God does, however, appear on the carved stone in the synagogue.

There were also ten specific rules given to Moses on two tablets of stone. These commandments are at the heart of Judaism and can be found above the ark in all synagogues today (see page 30).

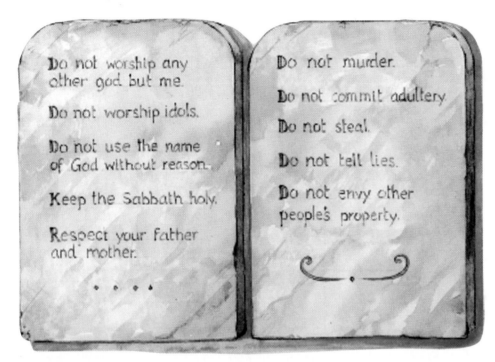

Do not worship any other god but me.

Do not worship idols.

Do not use the name of God without reason.

Keep the Sabbath holy.

Respect your father and mother.

Do not murder.

Do not commit adultery.

Do not steal.

Do not tell lies.

Do not envy other people's property.

Torah means the law or teachings. Jews believe these rules are contained in five books that God gave to Moses.

A **mitzvah** is a God-given commandment, or rule, in the Torah which Jews should obey. **Mitzvot** is the plural.

Orthodox Jews believe that all five books of the Torah today are word for word as God gave them to Moses. The contents of the Torah will last for ever and never become out of date. Reform Jews also accept that the Torah contains extremely important advice for living. Some Reform groups, however, think the Torah was inspired by God, but written by men over a long period of time. They argue that the information in the Torah was helpful for Jews living at the time when it was first written, but it may need interpreting for the modern world. All Jews accept that the Torah is the most important piece of Jewish scripture and the ultimate source of religious authority. Its importance to the Jews has led to them being called 'the people of the book'. Belief in the Torah has held the Jews together as a nation throughout history and today it plays a central part in their worship and code of conduct.

The Torah contains:

• accounts of God's involvement in history
• evidence of God's relationship with the Jews
• rules about how the Jews should live and worship.

Questions

1 What does the word 'Torah' mean?
2 How do Orthodox Jews believe the Torah was given to them?
3 Why do Jews think the Torah is more important than any other writings?
4 Explain the difference between the beliefs about the Torah of an Orthodox Jew and a Reform Jew.

Topic 3 Sources of authority

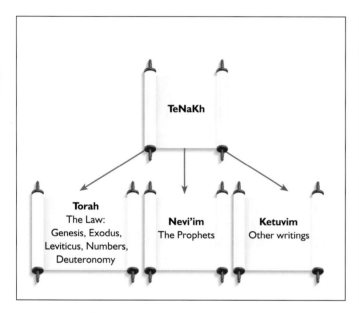

TeNaKh

Torah
The Law:
Genesis, Exodus,
Leviticus, Numbers,
Deuteronomy

Nevi'im
The Prophets

Ketuvim
Other writings

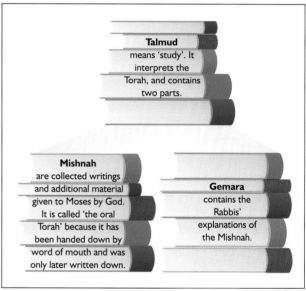

Talmud
means 'study'. It
interprets the
Torah, and contains
two parts.

Mishnah
are collected writings
and additional material
given to Moses by God.
It is called 'the oral
Torah' because it has
been handed down by
word of mouth and was
only later written down.

Gemara
contains the
Rabbis'
explanations of
the Mishnah.

What is...?

The **Tenakh** is
the name of the
Hebrew Bible.
It is made up of
three parts: the
Law, the Prophets,
and other writings.

Tenakh

The Jews' holy book is sometimes called the Hebrew Bible, but its correct name in Hebrew is the Tenakh. The Tenakh comprises three parts. The Torah is the first and most important section because it is believed to be the word of God and contains the rules about how Jews should lead their lives.

The next section is called the Nevi'im. This means the Prophets. Prophets are messengers sent to earth by God to teach people. The Nevi'im contains the writings of these people and the books are frequently named after them, e.g. Isaiah, Samuel and Amos.

Other sacred writings are grouped together in the section called the Ketuvim, which means 'other writings'. There are various scriptures in the Ketuvim but the best-loved book is the Psalms. This is a collection of 150 songs written by the great Jewish leader King David.

Whilst the Torah remains the most important part of the Tenakh and is used at all ceremonies, other parts are read on certain occasions. The book of Ruth in the Ketuvim, for instance, is read at the festival of Shavuot.

Students often work in pairs in a yeshiva debating the meaning of sections of the Talmud.

Talmud

Orthodox Jews believe that, in addition to the Torah, God explained to Moses in more detail how the commandments were to be kept. This information was carefully handed on by word of mouth and is known as the oral Torah, or Talmud. The Talmud comprises two parts: the written version (all 63 volumes of it) called the Mishnah, and further explanations called the Gemara. Some Jewish men take time off from everyday life to study the Talmud at a special college called a yeshiva.

Halakhah

The Halakhah is the Jewish law according to the Torah, built up over the centuries by learned rabbis. The Halakhah contains very detailed information about what is, and is not, permitted.

Jews believe that all the answers to life's problems can be found in the Torah but sometimes it requires scholars to study the text deeply in order to understand how it applies to a modern-day dilemma. What would be the Torah's attitude towards computer hacking? Is it acceptable for a Jew to receive an organ transplant from an animal? Is cloning permissible? These are only a few of the problems modern Jews face which would never have occurred at the time of Moses. Modern Jewish scholars study the Torah and Talmud to understand how their teachings apply to new problems. Eventually a Responsa is issued. This is an authoritative reply to the question.

Judgements about other legal or personal disputes according to Jewish law would be referred to a court of rabbis called the Bet Din. Further information about the Bet Din appears on page 33.

The **Talmud** is the oral Torah. It is made up of the **Mishnah** and the **Gemara**.

The **Responsa** are the up-to-date responses rabbis give to modern-day problems based on the teachings in the Torah.

1 Name the three books of the Tenakh.
2 What is the difference between the Torah and the Talmud?
3 Where would a Jewish student go to study the Talmud?
4 'Something written down thousands of years ago is no use for modern living.' What do you think? How would an Orthodox Jew respond to this remark?

Respect for the Torah

The Torah is carried shoulder-high to show the importance given to the word of God.

What is...?

A **sofer** is a scribe who writes the Torah scroll. He is an Orthodox Jewish man who has trained for seven years.

Great respect is shown to all Torah scrolls because they contain the word of God, but no scroll is ever worshipped. A Torah scroll is simply the carrier of divine words. Throughout its life a scroll will be accorded special attention from the moment ink first goes down on the parchment to its final disposal as a worn-out scroll.

A scroll must be written by a sofer, or scribe, who is an Orthodox Jewish man with seven years' training. A sofer must not be disturbed when he is writing because there must never be a mistake in the Torah. If he does make an error, that letter is scratched from the parchment with a knife, then written correctly. Should the mistake involve the name of God then the whole portion of parchment must be re-written because it is not permitted to deface such a holy name. A damaged section of parchment will be respectfully buried in the ground. (There are more details about the sofer's work on page 33.)

A scroll is stored with great care in the ark of the synagogue (see page 30). This is the holiest part of the synagogue because it contains the word of God. The scroll is wrapped in a velvet cover called the mantle. A silver ornament called a breastplate is hung over the mantle, and ornaments of crowns and bells are frequently placed on the top of the wooden rollers. Not only are these precious adornments but they also represent the kingship of the Torah.

When the Torah is to be read in the synagogue, the scroll is collected from the ark and carried in procession at shoulder-height to the bimah, the raised reading platform in the centre. Everyone stands and gives their full attention to the scroll. Some men standing close to the Torah as it passes may reach forward and touch the mantle with the fringe of their tallit (see page 27), then kiss its fringe as a sign of their love for the word of God.

It is an honour to be invited to stand in the bimah whilst the Torah is being read. An Orthodox Jewish man given that honour recites the words 'Pleased is he who has given the Torah' as he approaches the bimah. Because of the difficulties of chanting Hebrew, it is usually the chazan who reads from the Torah in an Orthodox service (see page 33).

No reader ever touches the words on the scroll with his finger when he is reading. Instead he uses a yad. This pointer is often shaped like a hand with a pointing finger, and it prevents sweat or grease from smudging the words of God and perhaps making them illegible.

After the reading, the Torah is carried all round the synagogue before it is put back in the ark. The scroll takes a longer route back to the ark than it did when it came out, symbolising the congregation's reluctance to put God's word away.

All scrolls are inspected regularly to ensure that the words remain legible. The word of God must be clear. The sofer will make repairs to small sections of parchment if necessary, but if a scroll becomes too worn or damaged then it is buried in a grave with due honour.

Activity

List as many different ways as you can in which Jews show respect for the Torah.

What is ...?

The **yad** is a metal pointer used for reading the Torah to prevent the writing being smudged or damaged by a person's finger.

 **Questions**

1 What is a yad and why is it used?
2 State two ways in which the importance of the Torah is shown to worshippers during the synagogue service.
3 What happens to damaged Torah scrolls?
4 How do Jews ensure that the words of the Torah are passed on accurately?

Topic 5 The Covenant

The **Covenant** is a promise. It refers to the special relationship between God and the Jewish people.

Jews believe that God made a special agreement with them long ago which is still in existence today. In ancient time God appeared to Abraham and told him:

I am the Almighty God. Obey me and always do what is right. ... I make this Covenant with you: I promise that you will be the ancestor of many nations... I will be your God and the God of your descendants. I will give to you and to your descendants this land.

(Genesis 17:1–2, 4, 7–8)

The Covenant is a deal which was struck between God and the Jews in ancient times. Jews believe it is still relevant today.

This means that the Jews must believe in one God and obey his commandments in the Torah. In return God promised to make them his chosen people and give them a land of their own. Jews believe that this land is modern-day Israel.

Now, if you will obey me and keep my Covenant, you will be my own people. The whole earth is mine, but you will be my chosen people, a people dedicated to me alone, and you will serve me as priests.

(Exodus 19:5–6)

As a sign the Jews agreed to the deal God demanded:

From now on you must circumcise every baby boy when he is eight days old... This will show that there is a Covenant between you and me.

(Genesis 17:11–12)

 What do you think?

What do you think the Jews mean when they speak of being 'the chosen people'? What might be the advantages and disadvantages of that?

This command to circumcise a Jewish baby boy has been carried out ever since (see page 54).

God repeated the terms of the Covenant he made with the Jews to Abraham's son Isaac, and his grandson, Jacob. God told Jacob:

> Remember, I will be with you and protect you wherever you go, and I will bring you back to this land. I will not leave you until I have done all that I have promised you.
>
> (Genesis 28:15)

There have been various times in their history when the Jews have been in difficulties. They believe that God has always come to their aid as he promised to. When the Jews were enslaved in Egypt, Moses turned to God for help and it was given. God told them:

> Now I have heard the groaning of the Israelites, whom the Egyptians have enslaved, and I remembered my Covenant. So tell the Israelites that I say to them, 'I am the Lord; I will rescue you and set you free from your slavery to the Egyptians.'
>
> (Exodus 6:5–6)

 **Activity**

Learn the terms of the Covenant.
God promised the Jews:
- God would give the Jews a land of their own
- God would take care of the Jews
- God would make the Jews his chosen people.

The Jews promised God:
- to obey God's commandments
- to circumcise all males at eight days old.

 **Questions**

1 What do Jews call their special relationship with God?
2 Name two things Jews believe God has promised their people.
3 What must Jews do to keep their side of the Covenant?
4 How is the Torah connected to the Covenant?

Do you understand...

Jewish beliefs and sources of authority?

Task 1

1 What is this scroll called?
2 Name four things you can identify in this picture.
3 Why is this scroll shown great respect?
4 Name the five books which make up the contents of this scroll.
5 Why do the Ten Commandments appear on the breastplate?

Task 2

1 What is the Mishnah?
2 What is the Gemara?
3 What is the difference between the Torah and the Talmud?

Task 3

'*You belong to the Lord your God; he has chosen you to be his own people from among all the peoples who live on earth.*' (Deuteronomy 14:2)

1 Jews believe they have a Covenant with God. What do they mean by that?
2 a What did God promise to do?
   b What did the Jews promise to do?

Task 4

'*Blessed be He who spoke and the world came into being; blessed be He. Blessed be He who maintains the creation.*' (Prayer Book)

1 What do Jews believe about God's part in Creation?
2 How can people play their part in this?
3 What do Jews mean when they speak of 'God the sustainer'?

Task 5

How many of these Hebrew terms can you define?

- Covenant
- Shema
- mitzvah
- yad
- Messianic Age
- mantle
- sofer
- Tenakh

Quick revision

- Jews believe in one God.
- The Torah contains the laws for living.
- The Covenant was an agreement between God and the Jews.
- The Shema is the declaration of faith in Judaism.

Topic 1

Daily prayer

Orthodox Jewish men are required to pray three times a day, in the morning, afternoon and evening. Prayers are said standing and facing towards Jerusalem. Women do not have set prayer times because this might cause difficulties if they have small children to look after, but they are expected to pray twice a day. Prayer is thought to help a Jew draw closer to God. Because Jews believe God will hear their prayers wherever they are said, daily prayer can take place anywhere. Home is a common place, not just because it is convenient, but because it is amongst the family. Most Jews try to attend synagogue for worship on Shabbat. Praying with others can be an uplifting experience for the individual and strengthen the religious commitment of the group.

Jews prepare for prayer by washing their hands as a sign of ritual purification. The head is covered as a sign of respect for God. A woman can wear any hat or scarf but a man usually puts on a small round cap called a kippah, or yamulkah. This can be any colour. Some Orthodox Jewish men and boys wear a kippah throughout the day as a constant reminder that God is higher than they are.

This Orthodox father dresses for morning prayer. His son is not yet Bar Mitzvah so he does not wear a tallit or tefillin.

What do you think?

'It doesn't matter what you wear to say prayers.' Do you agree? Give reasons for your answer, showing that you have considered both sides of the argument.

In the Torah God told Moses:

> *Make tassels on the corners of your garments and put a blue cord on each tassel. You are to do this for all time to come. The tassels will serve as reminders, and each time you see them you will remember all my commands and obey them.*
>
> (Numbers 15:38–39)

This has developed into the tallit, a large blue-and-white shawl of silk or wool. On the two ends are fringes and tassels representing the 613 rules the Torah commands a Jew to keep. A Jewish man says a brief blessing, then wraps the tallit around his shoulders for morning prayers to remind him that God surrounds him. Some Orthodox Jews wear the tallit katan, a short vest with tassels on the four corners, under their shirt throughout the day. The long tassels on each corner of the tallit have five knots in them, making ten on the left-hand side and ten on the right, symbolising the Ten Commandments. When they die, Jewish men are often buried with their tallit and the fringe is cut to show that they no longer have to keep the commandments.

Tefillin are put on for weekday prayer. These are two small black boxes, made from the leather of a kosher animal, which are strapped to the forehead and upper arm. They are a physical reminder of the Torah. By putting on tefillin, a Jewish man is fulfilling the command in the Shema:

> *Hear O Israel, the Lord our God is one God. Love the Lord your God with all your heart, with all your soul, and with all your strength. Never forget these commands that I am giving you today... Tie them on your arms and wear them on your foreheads as a reminder.*
>
> (Deuteronomy 6:4–8)

Inside the boxes are small pieces of parchment containing the whole of the Shema handwritten by a sofer, or scribe. Every three years the tefillin are opened by the sofer and checked to ensure that the writing is legible. The act of putting on the tallit and tefillin not only reminds Jews of their obligations to God, but also helps them to focus their mind on prayer. Reform Jews do not feel the need to wear these garments for prayer. The head tefillin reminds Jews to love God with all their mind. The arm tefillin symbolises loving God with all their strength.

 What is ...?

The **tefillin** are leather boxes worn on the head and arm for prayer.

What is ...?

The **kippah** or **yamulkah** is the name of the skull cap worn by Jewish boys and men.

What is ...?

The **tallit** is a fringed shawl worn by Jewish men, and some Reform women, for prayer.

Questions

1 When is a Jewish man commanded to pray?
2 Look at the words of the Shema and explain where the tefillin must be placed. What do those places symbolise?
3 Describe how an Orthodox Jewish man prepares for prayer and the reasons behind each of the garments.
4 How do these preparations help a Jew to pray?

Synagogue – function

3: Worship

 **What is...?**

The word **synagogue** means 'meeting place'. It is the name of the Jewish place of worship.

In ancient times the Jews' most sacred possessions were the two tablets of stone carrying the Ten Commandments that God gave to Moses. These stones were originally kept in a box called the aron hakodesh, or holy ark, and carried around by the Jews during their years in the desert. When they eventually settled in Israel the aron hakodesh was housed in the Temple in Jerusalem. Because of its precious contents, the Temple became the focal point for prayers. Today Jews still face that direction when they pray, and all synagogues are built facing Jerusalem.

Although Jews used to go to the Temple to offer sacrifice, most met in houses to study the Torah or to pray. The word 'synagogue' (from the Greek word *synago* meaning a 'meeting' or 'get-together') was used to describe these meetings. Some met outdoors – the Western Wall, the last remaining section of the original Temple in Jerusalem, is an open-air synagogue today.

LIME ROAD SYNAGOGUE

Weekly bulletin – events in the synagogue hall

LADIES' GUILD	8pm 3rd Wednesday in the month Next month's speaker on 'Cooking for Hanukkah'
SUNDAY SCHOOL	10am–1pm ages 5–12
TUESDAY CLUB	2pm 1st Tuesday in the month A friendship club for the retired Tea and a speaker
COUNCIL MEETINGS	8pm 1st Wednesday in the month For the men and women elected to run the synagogue
THURSDAY LUNCH	12.30am weekly All retired people welcome
SHIUR	Learn more about Judaism Every Tuesday 7.30–9pm (adult class) Every Monday 7.30–9pm (student class)
PLAYSCHOOL	Every morning 9–12 noon

The synagogue is the centre of Jewish community life. List the different events being held at this one, and against each say which part of the community is involved.

 What do you think?

Do you think it would matter to a Jewish family if they lived a long way from a synagogue?

The original meaning of the word synagogue is a useful reminder that the building has various purposes today which make it the centre of Jewish community life. Some of activities that take place there are sacred (religious) and some are secular (ordinary everyday things), showing that Judaism is as much a way of life as a religion.

What Is ...?

A **minyan** is a group of ten adult males who must be present for full synagogue worship to take place.

- **Worship** – the prayer hall is the most important part of the synagogue because the Torah scrolls are kept there. Listening to the Torah being read is considered a blessing and is only possible in a synagogue. Morning prayers may be said every day in the synagogue, although some Jews only attend on Shabbat. A minyan is a group of ten men who must be present in an Orthodox synagogue before a full service can take place. If there are fewer than ten, some parts of the service must be omitted.

- **Social** – the synagogue forms the heart of the community. There is often a hall at the side of the main building, where social events are held for all age groups, from mums and toddlers to elderly people. Celebrations of rites of passage may take place there. A family could have their baby son's Brit Milah in the hall, or their daughter's Bat Chayil, with a party to celebrate afterwards. Although a boy's Bar Mitzvah must take place in the prayer hall of the synagogue, the social hall could be used for the evening party or for a wedding reception.

- **Education** – Jewish people meet at the synagogue to study. Some Jews even use the old Yiddish word 'shul' for the synagogue, which gives a hint of its importance as a centre of learning. Some people go to learn more about the Torah, others Jewish history, the Hebrew language, or Jewish cookery. There are classes for children on Sunday mornings and special lessons for a young person studying to become Bar/ Bat Mitzvah or Bat Chayil. The synagogue is the place to go for advice. People can consult the rabbi about the teachings of the Torah concerning a religious problem, or an everyday issue such as whether a certain food is kosher.

There are no special features to distinguish the outside of a synagogue. Some may display a menorah design or a Star of David, but that is not necessary. The hall at the side acts as a community centre for the local Jewish population.

Questions

1 How does the word 'synagogue' get its meaning?
2 What is a minyan and why is it important in synagogue worship?
3 Explain the main functions of a synagogue.
4 'The synagogue is the focal point of the local Jewish community.' What does this mean? To what extent do you think this is true?

Topic 3

Synagogue – furnishings

What is ...?

The **ark** is the cupboard where the Torah scrolls are kept. It is the holiest part of the synagogue.
Ner tamid is the everlasting light symbolising the eternal presence of God.

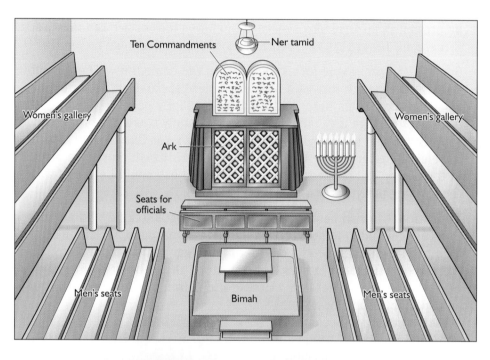

The most important part of the synagogue is the ark. Ner tamid hangs in front of the Ten Commandments above the ark.

The holiest area of the synagogue is the ark. It can be known by its Hebrew name aron hakodesh, which means sacred bookcase. The ark is a cupboard holding the Torah scrolls which Jews believe contain the words of God. To show how important the scrolls are, the ark is in a raised position on the wall facing Jerusalem and is reached by walking up steps. A curtain, called the parochet, is drawn across the closed doors of the ark, symbolically protecting the scrolls when they are not in use.

Above the ark hangs ner tamid, the eternal lamp. This light is kept burning to show the everlasting presence of God. Ner tamid reminds Jews of the menorah that burned in the original Temple.

Fixed to the wall above the ark are the Ten Commandments. These are the rules for life which God gave to Moses on two tablets of stone in Hebrew. Often only the opening words of each commandment appear in Hebrew on the synagogue stones because that is all there is space for.

In the middle of the synagogue is a raised platform called the bimah. On it there is a large desk where the Torah scroll can be unrolled for reading. The bimah is raised to demonstrate that the word of God is above people, but its position also makes it easy for people to see and hear what is being read. In some traditions the bimah is at the back of the synagogue and in others it is in a central position.

A seat and smaller reading-stand for the rabbi's prayer book are situated at the front near the ark. Officials who assist in the running of the synagogue, like the President and the Treasurer, have their own special seats below the bimah or at the side of the synagogue.

In an Orthodox synagogue men and women sit apart so that they will not distract each other during worship. Women sit in a gallery, or possibly in a separate section at the back, and do not take an active part in the conduct of the service. In a Reform synagogue men and women sit together and take an equal part in the service. The only music in an Orthodox synagogue is the human voice, but in a Reform synagogue there may be a musical instrument, such as an organ.

Pictures of humans are never found in a synagogue because the second of the Ten Commandments says, 'Do not worship idols'. If there is any decoration it will consist of patterns or landscapes.

? Questions

1 Which branch of Judaism requires men and women to sit apart during synagogue worship? Why?
2 List three ways in which respect is shown to the Torah in the synagogue.
3 Name the main features in a synagogue and explain their importance.
4 Explain the importance of ner tamid, the ark and the bimah.

Topic 4 Synagogue leaders

What is ...?

The **rabbi** is the teacher in the Jewish community and in the synagogue. He does not lead the service.
The **chazan** or **cantor** is the person responsible for leading synagogue worship.

The rabbi

The word 'rabbi' means teacher in Hebrew. One of the most important aspects of a rabbi's job is to know the Torah and the Halakhah (the Jewish law) well enough to assist people in the community to live their lives as God requires. Because this demands an extremely detailed knowledge and understanding of Judaism, a rabbi is usually a university graduate who has spent a further five years studying at a rabbinical college. Women are only permitted to become rabbis in Reform Judaism. Like the synagogue, the rabbi also has three functions: he is responsible for assisting with the education of his community, its worship, and pastoral care.

As part of his social and pastoral role, the rabbi not only conducts weddings and funerals but also gives guidance to those involved in either ceremony. He may also visit people who are ill at home or in hospital, or Jews in prison. The rabbi acts as a counsellor and may help Jewish students at a nearby university with their problems, as well as those in his synagogue community. Jews can ask their rabbi's advice about any aspect of life, ranging from whether a certain activity is acceptable on Shabbat to a personal problem that has arisen in a relationship, or a moral dilemma.

A rabbi also teaches people about Judaism. This might be through the sermon given in the synagogue or at special classes held in the week for children or adults. Boys preparing for their Bar Mitzvah are usually taught by the rabbi, as are girls preparing for their Bat Mitzvah in Reform Judaism.

The rabbi is an important person in the Jewish community because he is an expert in Jewish law. It is the chazan who actually leads synagogue worship.

Although the rabbi plays an important part in synagogue life, he does not need to be present for worship to take place. For this it is the minyan that is vital (see page 29). As an old Jewish saying puts it: 'Nine rabbis cannot make a minyan but ten shoemakers can.' In Reform Judaism a rabbi frequently does lead the synagogue service but in Orthodox Judaism he is not the leader. His role might be that of reading the sidra, the weekly passage from the Torah, or giving a sermon.

A rabbi may be part of a Bet Din. This is a court of three rabbis who rule on matters of Jewish law. Their duties involve deciding whether a couple can get divorced according to Jewish law, whether a person is suitably prepared for conversion to Judaism, or issuing kosher certification to a food manufacturer or retailer.

The chazan

The synagogue service is usually led by the chazan who chants prayers and portions of the Torah. He can also be known as the cantor. It is his singing that leads the congregation in worship, so a good voice is essential. The chazan stands in the bimah throughout the service and is easily recognised by his large hat. Training for this job is not just musical; the chazan receives instruction in the Torah, the prayer book and Jewish law. A chazan is important in the life of the synagogue. He is a paid employee and given the title Reverend. He knows all the chants by heart, and the correct order of services for Shabbat, festivals, weddings and Bar Mitzvahs. Some Reform synagogues no longer have a chazan. Instead the service is read in English by the rabbi, and musical instruments lead the singing. Others have a woman chazan.

The sofer

The scribe, known also by the Hebrew name sofer, does not work in the synagogue but he is a vital member of the synagogue community because he copies out the scrolls. A sofer is a religious man who has seven years' training in making the ink, preparing parchment and cutting quill pens, as well as writing Hebrew. He checks and repairs scrolls, from the tiny ones inside a mezuzah or tefillin to the large Torah scrolls used in the synagogue. The work of the sofer is very important – he must never be distracted in case he makes a mistake that would corrupt the scriptures.

Questions

1 Explain the job of the rabbi.
2 Would it be wrong to say that the rabbi leads synagogue service?
3 Do you think a synagogue community would lose out very much if they could not afford to employ their own rabbi?

Do you understand...
worship in Judaism?

Task 1

1. Name three items which an Orthodox Jewish man puts on for prayer.
2. What is the meaning of the leather boxes and straps he wears on his head and arms?
3. 'A religious believer must pray every day.' Do you agree? Explain your reasons and show that you have considered another point of view.

Task 2

1. Is this rabbi Orthodox or Reform? How do you know?
2. State two ways in which a rabbi serves the community.
3. Describe the role of the chazan in the synagogue.
4. How has Reform Judaism changed the role of women in the synagogue?

3: Worship

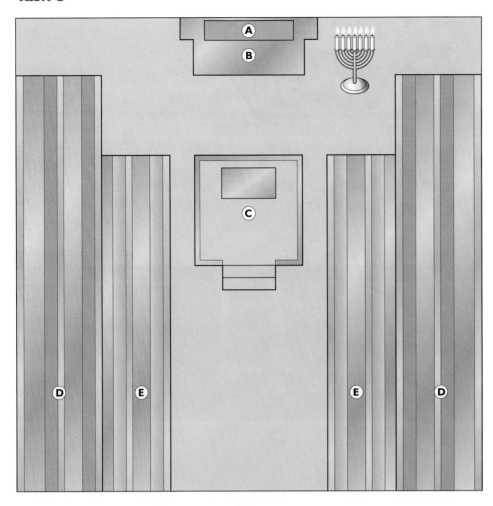

Task 3

1 Name A, B, C and D in this synagogue.
2 Explain their significance.
3 'It is the synagogue that keeps the Jewish community together.'
  Do you agree? State your reasons and show that you have considered another point of view.

Task 4

How many of these Hebrew terms can you define?
* ner tamid • tefillin • kippah • ark • parochet • minyan
* chazan • bimah • sofer • tallit • Bet Din • aron hakodesh

✓ Quick revision

* 'Synagogue' means meeting place.
* The ark is the holiest place in the synagogue because it holds the Torah.
* A synagogue is used for worship, education and social events.
* The chazan leads the worship in a synagogue.

Topic 1

Shabbat – Friday preparations

Each item on the Shabbat table has a religious significance, even the challah cover. Not only does it keep the bread clean but it also reminds Jews of the dew that landed on the manna when their ancestors were wandering in the desert.

Shabbat is the most important festival in Judaism because it occurs every week. It is the Jewish day of rest that is commanded in the Torah. It is the fourth of the Ten Commandments:

Observe the Sabbath and keep it holy, as I, the Lord your God, have commanded you. You have six days in which to do your work, but the seventh day is a day of rest dedicated to me. On that day no one is to work – neither you, your children, your slaves, your animals, nor the foreigners who live in your country... Remember that you were slaves in Egypt, and that I, the Lord your God, rescued you by my great power and strength. That is why I command you to observe the Sabbath.

(Deuteronomy 5:12–15)

Shabbat begins at sunset on Friday and from then on no work is done until Shabbat ends at sunset on Saturday. Days are counted from sunset to sunset in Judaism because Genesis 1:5 says: *'Evening passed and morning came – that was the first day.'* Because Shabbat is such a holy day there are major preparations. House-cleaning, shopping, cooking and table-laying must all be finished before sunset. Everyone in the family arrives home in time to wash and change ready to welcome Shabbat in.

Immediately before sunset it is customary for the mother in the family to cover her head and light two candles, one for each command in the Torah to celebrate Shabbat. She beckons the light towards her and recites a blessing over her children.

The father frequently welcomes Shabbat at synagogue which he attends with his sons. When they return, the family sit down together to share the Shabbat meal, the best meal of the week. At the table the father opens the meal with a blessing, the Kiddush, said over a goblet of red wine. He sips the wine, a symbol of celebration, and passes the goblet to everyone else to take a sip. Then he says a blessing over two loaves of bread called challah. These loaves are a reminder to Jews of one of the many times in their history when God took care of them. When they were wandering in the desert God sent them food every day. On the sixth day he sent a double portion so that they could rest on the seventh day. At the Shabbat meal one challah loaf is cut and frequently sprinkled with a little salt, before pieces are passed around for everyone to eat. In the past salt was so expensive it was only used on Shabbat, demonstrating that the best was reserved for God's holy day.

The atmosphere at Shabbat is one of leisurely enjoyment. After the ceremony with wine and bread the family eat their supper. This may be the only day in the week when some families are able to share a meal together and spend time in each other's company. As such Shabbat is valued. Some Orthodox families sing special Shabbat songs during the evening and tell children stories from Jewish history. At the conclusion of the meal a special grace is recited.

One learned rabbi said: *'Israel has kept Shabbat, but Shabbat has kept Israel.'* He meant that because the Jews have celebrated Shabbat in the same way for centuries this weekly celebration has held them together as a nation.

What is …?

The **Kiddush** is a blessing said over a cup of red wine at the Shabbat meal.

Questions

1 When does Shabbat **a** begin **b** end?
2 Describe how a Jewish woman welcomes the beginning of Shabbat.
3 Explain what happens at the Friday evening meal, and its religious significance.
4 'Staying in on Friday night is nothing but a bore.' How do you think an Orthodox Jewish mother would reply to her teenage daughter?

Topic 2

Shabbat – Saturday observance

What is the meaning of the three items used to celebrate havdalah?

What do you think?

What difference would it make to your weekend if you were Jewish? Why would a Jew consider these changes worthwhile? Do you think you would gain anything?

Shabbat celebrates God's creation of the world.

In six days I, the Lord, made the earth, the sky, the sea, and everything in them, but on the seventh day I rested. That is why I, the Lord, blessed the Sabbath and made it holy.

(Exodus 20:11)

Shabbat continues as a day of rest until Saturday sunset. The Torah lists 39 activities that Jews are forbidden to do during Shabbat. The intention is that Shabbat will be one day in the week when everybody can have a break, spend time with the family and study the Torah. Many of the forbidden tasks, like ploughing and weaving, would make little difference to a modern Jew. It is the command not to kindle fire that has the greatest impact. Orthodox rabbis have interpreted this to forbid any activity that would create a spark, which means not using electricity. An Orthodox Jew is not allowed to switch on any electrical appliance during Shabbat, nor a car engine. Today a modern Orthodox Jew uses an electronic timer to ensure that lights, heating and cooking appliances come on by themselves, but a car is not used except in an emergency. The Torah makes it clear that saving the life of a person or an animal always comes first; Shabbat rules can be broken if necessary.

On Saturday morning it is usual for the whole family to attend the synagogue service. Orthodox Jews will only be able to go to synagogue if it is a short walk away but Reform Jews are prepared to drive if necessary.

At Saturday sunset the family meet together to bid farewell to the holy day. The ceremony is called havdalah, which means 'separation', because it marks the separation of the holy day from the rest of the week. At sunset, the father lights a havdalah candle. This plaited candle has several wicks and creates a blaze of light to show that Shabbat is over and fire may now be lit. The father says a blessing over a goblet of wine which everyone sips, then he says a blessing over a spice box. Each person sniffs the spice box as it is passed around. This symbolises the hope that the sweetness of Shabbat will last into the new week. Everybody wishes each other a good week as they sing a final hymn. The havdalah candle is ceremonially snuffed out in a saucer of wine.

Non-Jews sometimes find it hard to understand why Jewish people look forward to Shabbat. To some it seems like 24 hours when you can't do anything. Jews would say it is a treat, a holiday – a word that originally meant 'holy day'. Shabbat is the one day a week when everyone in the family has time to see and talk to each other. Some might call it 'quality time'. It is an opportunity to relax away from the stresses of the working day. Because food preparations and cleaning are done ahead, it is even a day off for the person who runs the house. Jews say that is real freedom. They remember that in ancient times when they were slaves in Egypt, they never had such freedom. The Torah states clearly that everyone is entitled to one day a week of rest, even slaves and working animals.

What is …?

The ceremony to end Shabbat is called **havdalah**. It marks the separation of the holy day from the rest of the week.

Questions

1 What is the name of the ceremony that closes Shabbat?

2 Explain why Jews do not work on Shabbat.

3 Describe the ceremony that ends Shabbat and explain its religious significance.

4 'Keeping Shabbat is old-fashioned and out of place in today's busy world.' Do you agree? Explain your answer, and show that you have considered more than one point of view.

Topic 3 Rosh Hashanah

Rosh Hashanah is the Jewish New Year, which lasts for ten days.

The **shofar** is a ram's horn that is blown in the synagogue during the ten days of Rosh Hashanah. It calls people to repent.

For Jews the new year is a time for new beginnings; a time to reflect on past mistakes and an opportunity to do better. For this reason, Rosh Hashanah is a holy time when Jews think about the beginning and end of the world; it is the anniversary of Creation and a reminder of the Day of Judgement. Although this is a very serious time, it is a holiday and Jews send each other new year cards. In some cards there is the greeting *'May you be inscribed in the Book of Life'*. This refers to a belief that on the first day of Rosh Hashanah, God opens a book with everyone's names in it and makes decisions about their future destiny. At the end of the ten-day period, the book is closed and a person's fate is sealed for the next twelve months. By spending these ten days reflecting on past mistakes and trying to make amends, Jews hope that God will forgive them.

It is commanded in the scriptures that the shofar must be blown at new year: *'On the first day of the seventh month you are to gather for worship, and no work is to be done. On that day trumpets are to be blown.'* (Numbers 29:1)

Bread is thrown into running water in the ceremony of Taslich. This symbolically enacts the words of the prophet Micah: *'You will trample our sins underfoot and sent them to the bottom of the sea!'* (Micah 7:19)

The shofar is blown in the synagogue. In ancient times this stirring sound called people into battle or announced important occasions. It was said to be sounded at the creation of the world and when Moses was given the Torah on Mount Sinai. It is blown on the first day of Rosh Hashanah to wake people up to repentance, and sounded throughout the ten days of this festival.

On the first evening, people often dress in new clothes as a sign of a new beginning. When the father and sons return from synagogue, the family sit down to a traditional Rosh Hashanah meal. The challah loaf is often round, symbolising the unbroken cycle of life and the hope that everyone in the family will have a full new year. Honey is on the table to wish everyone a sweet new year. Some people will eat honey cake or pieces of apple dipped in honey. Apples are used especially because their round shape has the same meaning as the challah. Pomegranates are another traditional fruit because it is said there are 613 seeds in a pomegranate, one for each of the 613 commandments a Jew must keep. A fish head, or cooked fish with its head on, is also traditional on the Rosh Hashanah table. The wish is that everyone's good deeds will multiply like the fish in the sea.

During the afternoon of the following day, some Jews go down to a river or some flowing water for the ceremony called Taslich, which means 'casting away'. People empty the crumbs and fluff from their pockets into the water. Others break little pieces of bread which they throw on the water as a ritual way of washing away their sins.

During the ten days of Rosh Hashanah, Jews make an effort to think about things they have done wrong during the previous year. This is the time to settle arguments and apologise for hurtful comments. Equally it is a time to accept others' apologies and put an end to grudges.

Questions

1 What is celebrated at Rosh Hashanah?
2 What are Jews expected to do during the ten days of Rosh Hashanah?
3 What is a shofar and how is it used at this festival?
4 Choose three customs followed by Jews during Rosh Hashanah and explain their significance.
5 'Rosh Hashanah is hardly a holiday.' Do you agree? Give reasons for your answer, showing that you have considered more than one point of view.

Topic 4

Yom Kippur

At Yom Kippur some Jews dress in white to show God they wish for purity. This man is wearing a kittel.

What is ...?

Yom Kippur is the Day of Atonement. This is the last of the ten days of Jewish new year, and the holiest day in the calendar.

> The tenth day of the seventh month is the day when the annual ritual is to be performed to take away the sins of the people. On that day do not eat anything at all; come together for worship... Do not work on that day, because it is the day for performing the ritual to take away sin. Anyone who eats anything on that day will no longer be considered one of God's people. And if anyone does any work on that day, the Lord himself will put him to death. This regulation applies to all your descendants, no matter where they live. From sunset on the ninth day of the month to sunset on the tenth observe this day as a special day of rest, during which nothing may be eaten.
>
> (Leviticus 23:26–32)

Yom Kippur means Day of Atonement, or repentance, and is the holiest day of the year. It is the day when Jews confess to God what they have done wrong during the previous year.

> This ritual must be performed once a year to purify the people of Israel from all their sins.
>
> (Leviticus 16:34)

A shofar, or ram's horn, is blown to summon people to repentance. Because the observance of Yom Kippur is commanded several times in the Torah, all Jews treat the day seriously. No one goes to work or school.

- Fasting – All adult Jews who are fit and healthy do not eat or drink anything for 25 hours from sunset to sunset. This is to show God that they sincerely wish for forgiveness and can discipline their body to concentrate on spiritual matters. For the same reason no one has sex during Yom Kippur. This is a time to think about God, not yourself. In the week before Yom Kippur food or money is donated to charity.

- No leather shoes – Jews give up wearing leather shoes to show their rejection of personal luxury and comfort.

- No anointing – No make-up, perfumes or jewellery are worn on this day. Jews come before God as they really are.

- Wearing white clothes – In the book of Isaiah 1:18 it says, *'You are stained red with sin, but I will wash you as clean as snow. Although your stains are deep red, you will be as white as wool.'* Orthodox Jews put on white clothes to symbolise their wish for purity.

- Remembering the dead – Jahrzeit candles are lit and burn throughout Yom Kippur. Jews recite a special prayer remembering those who have died.

- Synagogue attendance – All Jews try to attend synagogue for the evening prayers, even those who never go to synagogue at other times. Those who cannot attend synagogue spend the whole day in quiet thought.

The synagogue is open throughout Yom Kippur and some people stay there for the whole time. The doors of the ark are left open to symbolise the Jews' openness to repentance. White is seen on the robes of the rabbi and chazan, the parochet and Torah mantles. Before the evening service begins the chazan chants a special prayer called Kol Nidrei which asks God to release them from any false promises. The most important part of the service is the confession everyone recites together. Readings from the Torah at this time remind Jews how their ancestors sent a goat into the desert to symbolically carry away everyone's sins. The book of Jonah tells of God's forgiveness for those who truly repent. The service ends with the first line of the Shema, and a final blast from the shofar lets everyone know Yom Kippur has ended.

 **Questions**

1 What does 'Yom Kippur' mean?
2 Yom Kippur is a very serious time. State three ways in which Jews show sorrow and repentance on this occasion.
3 'Yom Kippur is the holiest day of the Jewish year, but being sorry for your sins on only one day each year is not enough.' Do you agree? Give reasons for your answer, showing that you have considered more than one point of view.

Topic 5 Hanukkah

What is...?

The mid-winter festival of **Hanukkah** is also called the Festival of Lights. Hanukkah is a time when Jews rededicate themselves to God.

A nine-branch candlestick is called a hanukiah. The central servant candle is used to light one more candle on each of the eight nights of Hanukkah.

Inside this Hanukkah card it says: *'May the happiness of Hanukkah stay with you all the year and the strength of the Maccabees always be near.'* What does that refer to?

We light these lights on account of the miracles, the deliverances and the wonders which You performed for our fathers by means of Your holy priests. Throughout the eight days of Hanukkah these lights are sacred; and we are not permitted to make any other use of them, except to look at them, in order to sing praises to Your name for Your miracles, Your deliverances and Your wonders.

(from the Hanukkah service)

Hanukkah is not a major religious festival but it is very popular because it involves sending cards and giving presents to children. It comes in the winter months and the evenings are brightened by candlelight, so the festival is often called the Festival of Lights.

What do you think?

'Festivals like Hanukkah are only for kids.' Do you agree, or could Hanukkah have any meaning for adults?

As with many Jewish festivals, Hanukkah remembers an important event in Jewish history that has lessons for Jews today. They remember how God took care of them and they kept their religion going despite strong opposition. Hanukkah is the time for Jews to rededicate themselves to God in the same way that their Temple was cleansed and rededicated to God.

The Hanukkah story

Around 175 BCE the Jewish homeland was occupied by the Syrians and ruled harshly by Antiochus. He tried to stamp out Judaism by banning many religious practices and forcing the Jews to do things that were forbidden, like eating pork and worshipping statues. Some Jews bravely refused and were killed. Another small group of Jewish freedom fighters led by Judas the Maccabee (his name means 'the hammer'!) fought back. Eventually they defeated the Syrians and regained control of their Temple in Jerusalem. It was in an appalling state but they cleaned it and prepared to rededicate it to God. Judas' men could only find one uncontaminated jar of oil to light the Temple menorah. Unfortunately this would only be sufficient to keep the menorah burning for one day, and it would take eight days before more oil could be prepared. However, the High Priest lit the menorah and, it is said, the menorah miraculously burned for eight days until the new oil arrived.

Today Hanukkah is celebrated with a nine-branch menorah called a hanukiah. It has eight branches to remember the eight days when the Temple menorah burned, and one other branch which is the servant candle. The servant is used to light the other candles, rather like a pilot light. On the first night of Hanukkah the servant candle lights the first candle and both are allowed to burn for about half an hour. On the second evening the servant candle lights two candles, and so on. On the eighth and final night, the whole hanukiah is a blaze of light. The candlestick is often stood on a windowsill so that its light can be seen outside as a sign of the power of good over evil and light over darkness. These lights have special significance, so no one should use them to light something else like a cigarette or a fire.

Children love Hanukkah because they are given small presents of money each evening after the lighting of the hanukiah. It is a time for playing traditional games – a favourite one involves a four-sided spinning top called a dreidel. Foods eaten at Hanukkah are cooked in oil to recall the miracle of the oil in the Temple. Doughnuts and fried latkes or potato cakes are especially popular.

Questions

1 Why is Hanukkah called the Festival of Lights?
2 State two ways in which the modern festival of Hanukkah remembers the old story.
3 Explain what the coloured parts of the quotation on page 44 refer to.

Preparations for Pesach

A Pesach card.

What is...?

Pesach is a festival that celebrates the Jews' freedom from slavery. It is also called Passover.

Pesach is a major Jewish festival that is also known as Passover. Pesach is essentially a celebration of freedom. The story connected with Pesach concerns the rescue of the Jews from Egyptian slavery around 1200 BCE, but the festival celebrates all the other times God has saved the Jews from their enemies.

The Exodus story

The Jews were captured by the Egyptians and made to build pyramids and other buildings. They tried to regain their freedom but failed until Moses became their leader. He decided to ask God for assistance. God helped them by sending ten horrific plagues on the Egyptians, each worse than the last. On the evening before the tenth plague, God gave the Jews specific instructions:

...each man must choose either a lamb or a young goat for his household... Then, on the evening of the fourteenth day of the month, the whole community of Israel will kill the animals. The people are to take some of the blood and put it on the doorposts and above the doors of the houses in which the animals are to be eaten. That night the meat is to be roasted, and eaten with bitter herbs and with bread made without yeast... You must not leave any of it until morning; if any is left over, it must be burnt. You are to eat it quickly, for you are to be dressed for travel, with your sandals on your feet and your stick in your hand. It is the Passover Festival to honour me, the Lord.

(Exodus 12:3–11)

What do you think?

Do you think there is anything to be gained by re-enacting something that happened 3,000 years ago?

4: Jewish festivals

The festival was called Pesach (in English, Passover) because that night the angel of death passed over the Jews' houses marked with blood but went into the houses of the Egyptians who had not marked their doorposts. As a result the eldest son in every Egyptian house was killed, and the distraught Egyptians kicked the Jews out of the country. Without God's intervention, the Jews believe they would never have escaped.

God commanded them:

> *You must celebrate this day as a religious festival to remind you of what I, the Lord, have done. Celebrate it for all time to come.*
>
> (Exodus 12:14)

Today Pesach is a major festival in the Jewish calendar, which requires careful preparation.

> *On the first day you are to get rid of all the yeast in your houses, for if anyone during those seven days eats bread made with yeast, he shall no longer be considered one of my people.*
>
> (Exodus 12:15)

This command is taken seriously. The house is spring-cleaned thoroughly in the week before Pesach, with particular attention paid to the kitchen. Remembering how their ancestors made bread without yeast since there was no time for it to rise, modern Jews remove every trace of yeast from their house for the eight days of Pesach. Besides bread this involves removing lots of other foods containing flour, like cakes, biscuits, pasta, some crisps, cereal – and even drinks like beer and whisky, which have yeast in them. Orthodox Jews follow the command strictly and these foods are often 'sold' to a non-Jewish neighbour then bought back after Pesach. Reform Jews are more likely to box these items up and put them in a cupboard or garage until the end of the festival. New food guaranteed never to have had contact with yeast is bought for Pesach. Young children learn about removing yeast, in the form of a game. Their father usually hides ten bread crumbs, known as chametz, and they have to search for them so that the crumbs can be ceremonially burned. All cooking utensils and crockery that have been in contact with yeast during the year are put away for Pesach. Another set of crockery, utensils and cutlery, kept exclusively for Pesach, is brought out.

What is …?

Crumbs that are swept up and burned before Pesach are called **chametz**. This is done to clear the house of all yeast.

Questions

1 What does Pesach celebrate?
2 Describe the historical events remembered at Pesach.
3 Why do Jews go to such lengths to get rid of yeast during Pesach?

Topic 7

Pesach and the seder meal

Pesach lasts for eight days but the first night of Pesach is the most important one. It is celebrated by a ritual meal at home called the seder meal. Everyone makes a big effort to return home for this family meal, even if they live away from home. This is the family event of the year. Men attend evening prayers at the synagogue whilst the women in the family lay the seder table with great care, beginning with a white cloth and two candlesticks. Cushions are put on everyone's chair so they can be comfortable and can take their time over the meal. This is a sign of freedom which slaves are not permitted. The small booklet called the Hagadah is put by everyone's place so that they can follow the traditional words of the ceremony.

Each person is given a wine glass, and an extra glass is placed on the table for the prophet Elijah. It is said he will return one day to bring in a Messianic Age (see page 15). Other traditions say he visits every house at Pesach. Some Jews even get up during the meal and open the front door to show their readiness to welcome the prophet back. On the Pesach table several bottles of wine are put ready for the meal. The father will say kiddush, or blessing, over the first cup of wine, and during the meal each person will drink four glasses of wine (or maybe just four sips) to remember the four promises God made to the Jews:

Everything on the seder table has a symbolic meaning. Can you identify the foods on the seder plate?

- I will bring you out.
- I will deliver you.
- I will redeem you.
- I will take you to Me.

Wine is also used in the seder service to make ten drips onto a table napkin, recalling the ten plagues God imposed on the Egyptians.

Bread made without yeast goes on the table. It is called matzah and looks like cracker biscuits. Three matzot are put under a cover on the festive table. The first two pieces will be blessed and eaten. Pieces of the third one, called afikomen, are hidden for the children to find. Each person eats a small piece of afikomen at the end of the meal as the very last food of the seder meal.

Matzah is bread made without yeast that is used throughout the eight days of Pesach. (*Matzah* is the Hebrew singular, and *matzot* is the plural form.)

The seder plate goes in the centre of the table. It will have on it these items:

- A roasted shank-bone, which is not eaten but is a reminder of the lamb killed at the first Pesach.

- Bitter herbs – usually horseradish which tastes so strong it makes the eyes water, reminding Jews of the bitterness of slavery.

- Charoset, a sweet paste made from apples, wine and nuts. It makes Jews think about the sweetness of their freedom. It looks like the mortar slaves used to cement Egyptian buildings together.

- A roasted egg – this is not eaten but symbolises the burnt offering once made in the Temple. Eggs are a symbol of new life.

- A green vegetable, called by the Hebrew name karpas. It is often lettuce or parsley, whose greenness is a reminder that this is a spring festival. The green vegetable is dipped in salt water (a symbol of the tears slaves shed) and eaten.

When everyone returns from synagogue the meal begins. The youngest child has the honour of beginning the ceremony by asking the traditional question: *'Why is this night different from all other nights?'* This will lead into a retelling of the Exodus story and the meaning of the traditional foods on the seder plate. A full meal follows this Pesach ceremony and the evening usually ends with traditional songs.

Questions

1 What does the word 'seder' mean?
2 Name two symbolic foods used at Pesach and explain their meaning.
3 How does this festival show the importance of the family?
4 How are Jews reminded at Pesach of their slavery and the exodus from Egypt?

Topic 8 — Shavuot and Sukkot

Shavuot is a harvest festival that celebrates the giving of the Torah to Moses on Mount Sinai.

Pesach, Shavuot and Sukkot are known as the pilgrim festivals because in ancient times men were commanded to make a pilgrimage up to the Temple in Jerusalem at these times to offer the first fruits of their harvest.

> All the men of your nation are to come to worship the Lord three times a year at the one place of worship: at Passover, Harvest Festival and the Festival of Shelters. Each man is to bring a gift as he is able, in proportion to the blessings that the Lord your God has given him.
>
> **(Deuteronomy 16:16–17)**

Shavuot

Shavuot comes seven weeks after Pesach and is also called the Festival of Weeks.

> Count seven weeks from the time that you begin to harvest the corn, and then celebrate the Harvest Festival, to honour the Lord your God, by bringing him a freewill offering in proportion to the blessing he has given you.
>
> **(Deuteronomy 16:9–10)**

Today this link with the harvest can be seen in the way synagogues are decorated with flowers and plants as a sign of thanksgiving to God. The festival also celebrates the giving of the Torah to Moses and the Jewish nation. On the eve of the festival some men spend the whole night studying the scriptures in honour of the Torah. At synagogue next morning the readings from Exodus describe Moses ascending Mount Sinai to receive the Ten Commandments. The other reading is a harvest one taken from the Book of Ruth. Ruth was not born Jewish but is greatly respected because she converted to Judaism and showed great honour and devotion to the Torah. She also became the great-grandmother of King David, whose birth and death are said to have occurred at Shavuot.

The stained-glass window is decorated with images of harvest.

The two-day festival of Shavuot is celebrated in the home with dairy products and honey. This remembers Israel as *'a land flowing with milk and honey'* and the Torah *'as sweet as honey and as nourishing as milk'* to those who study it. Round loaves decorated with a ladder design are baked to symbolise Moses ascending Mount Sinai to receive the Torah.

Sukkot

This festival has the name Festival of Shelters or Tabernacles. It commemorates the 40 years when Moses led the Jews through the Sinai desert and they had only simple shelters to live in. Today Jews construct a basic hut called a sukkah (*sukkot* is the plural) in their garden. The sides can be made of anything, but the roof must be made of branches with enough spaces between to see the sky and let in the rain! The Torah commands:

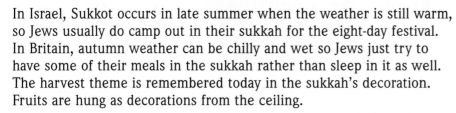

All the people of Israel shall live in shelters for seven days, so that your descendants may know that the Lord made the people of Israel live in simple shelters when he led them out of Egypt.

(Leviticus 23:42–43)

In Israel, Sukkot occurs in late summer when the weather is still warm, so Jews usually do camp out in their sukkah for the eight-day festival. In Britain, autumn weather can be chilly and wet so Jews just try to have some of their meals in the sukkah rather than sleep in it as well. The harvest theme is remembered today in the sukkah's decoration. Fruits are hung as decorations from the ceiling.

The Torah commands that a wand, called a lulav, be made from stems of palm, willow and myrtle. This should be waved in all directions to demonstrate to all that God's blessings are spread to all corners of the world.

What is…?

Jews are reminded that they depend on God for protection at the festival of **Sukkot**.

Questions

1 Which are the three pilgrim festivals? How do they get this name?
2 What part of the Jews' history is remembered at Sukkot?
3 What scripture passages are read at Shavuot, and why?
4 'Jewish festivals are just an excuse for eating and drinking.' Would you agree, or could they have a deeper meaning?

Do you understand...
Jewish festivals?

Task 1

1 Why is Shabbat important to Jews?
2 Give an account of how Shabbat is celebrated in the home.
3 Explain how and why Reform Jews might differ from Orthodox Jews in the way they keep Shabbat.
4 What problems do you think an Orthodox Jew might have in keeping Shabbat in Britain today?

Task 2

1 What is the serious message behind the festivities at Hanukkah?
2 Which are the pilgrim festivals and how do they get their name?
3 'Rosh Hashanah should be more important to Jews than any other festival.' Do you agree? Explain your answer, showing that you have considered other points of view.

Task 3

1 At which festival do Jews eat a seder meal?
2 Name the foods that appear on this seder plate.
3 Explain the meaning of each one.

Task 4

1 What is this hut called?
2 Why is it built?
3 What do Jews remember at this festival?
4 'There is no point is celebrating the same festival every year – it gets boring.' What do you think? Give reasons for your answer, and consider how a Jew might answer.

Task 5

Choose three pictures. State which festival each one matches, and explain its meaning.

Task 6

How many of these Hebrew words can you define?
- afikomen
- lulav
- hanukiah
- matzot
- sukkah
- Taslich
- seder
- chametz

Quick revision

- Rosh Hashanah lasts 10 days.
- Yom Kippur means Day of Atonement.
- Pesach celebrates the Jews' freedom from slavery.
- Shabbat lasts from sunset on Friday to sunset on Saturday.

Topic 1

Birth and Brit Milah

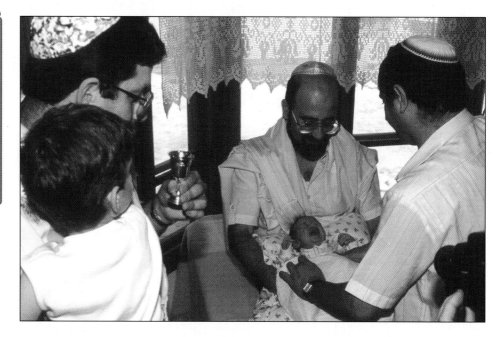

The sandek is a friend or relative given the honour of holding the baby during the circumcision.

> God said to Abraham: 'From now on you must circumcise every baby boy when he is eight days old... This will show that there is a covenant between you and me. Each one must be circumcised, and this will be a physical sign to show that my Covenant with you is everlasting.'
>
> (Genesis 17:9–13)

As a sign of the Covenant (see page 22), God required all baby boys to be circumcised at eight days old. This tradition continues to the present day, unless the baby is not well enough for the operation. Circumcision is usually carried out at home with family and friends present to celebrate, but it can take place in hospital.

On the eighth day the baby boy is carried into the room by a chosen friend or relative and those assembled say: 'Blessed is he who comes'. Women are not allowed in the room during the operation. The baby is handed over to the mohel. He is an Orthodox Jew who is specially trained in religious circumcision but not necessarily a doctor. It is traditional for the mohel to place the child for a brief moment on an empty chair. This chair is called Elijah's chair and reminds Jews that the prophet Elijah is said to be present in spirit at every circumcision. The baby is then placed on a cushion on the lap of the sandek, the man who will hold the baby during the operation. The sandek may be a special friend of the father, or a respected relative. The operation to remove the boy's foreskin is carried out swiftly and without anaesthetic. The mohel puts a dressing on the wound which will heal within days.

On completion the father recites the Benediction:

> *Blessed are You O Lord our God, King of the universe, who has sanctified us with His commandments, and has commanded us to bring our son into the Covenant of Abraham, our father.*

The mohel says a blessing over a goblet of wine, the sign of celebration, and names the child. Wine is sipped by the sandek, and a few drops are dripped onto the baby's tongue. The wine is handed to the mother to drink so that she can share in the celebration as her baby is handed back to her for a cuddle. Everyone enjoys a festive meal to celebrate this significant day.

Redemption of the firstborn son

> *The Lord said to Moses, 'Dedicate all the firstborn males to me... but... you must buy back every firstborn male child of yours.'*
>
> (Exodus 13:1 and 13)

Some Orthodox families have a ceremony at home when the baby boy is 30 days old. The father offers five silver coins to a member of the Cohen family, symbolically buying back his little son from priestly duties. (The Cohen families of today are descendants of the original priests in the Temple.) A blessing is said and a meal shared.

The baby girl's ceremony

The birth of a Jewish girl is marked in the synagogue. On the Shabbat following her birth, the father is honoured by being called to the bimah for the reading of the Torah. The name of his new daughter is announced and the rabbi says a blessing. In some Reform communities both parents take their baby daughter to the synagogue for the blessing. Family and friends often celebrate the occasion with a small party.

? Questions

1 How is a baby girl given her name?
2 How is the circumcision ceremony connected with the Covenant?
3 Explain the roles of the sandek and the mohel.
4 Why do you think a Jewish family believes it is important to hold a Brit Milah?
5 Describe the birth and Brit Milah ceremonies for Jewish children.

Topic 2

Bar Mitzvah and Bat Chayil

What is...?

Bar Mitzvah means 'son of the commandments'. It is used when a 13-year-old boy takes responsibility for his religious life.

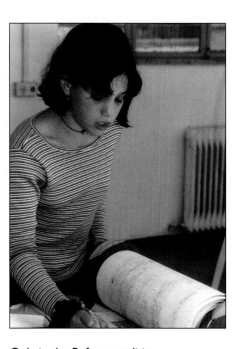

Being called out to read from the Torah is a great responsibility for a 13-year-old boy. It is also an awesome experience.

Only in the Reform tradition can a girl have a similar ceremony to a boy. This is called Bat Mitzvah.

What is...?

An Orthodox Jewish girl comes of age at 12, in a ceremony called **Bat Chayil**, literally meaning 'daughter of worth'.

The father is responsible for ensuring that his son performs his religious duties, up to the age of 13. The scriptures say, *'Thirteen is the age for the fulfilment of the commandments'*, and the ceremony to mark this is called Bar Mitzvah. The Hebrew words mean 'son of the commandments'. In the year before his Bar Mitzvah a boy has to learn Hebrew so that he can read aloud his portion of the Torah in the synagogue. He also has to learn to put on the tefillin, the tallit and kippah which he must wear for morning prayer from now on (see page 26). The rabbi will also teach him about other

What do you think?

As part of the Bar Mitzvah ceremony the father says: *'Blessed is the One who has freed me from responsibility for the boy's sins.'* What do you think he means?

religious duties, like keeping the Yom Kippur fast. Once a boy has come of age, he can be counted part of the minyan, the group of ten adult males necessary for synagogue prayers (see page 29).

Although a boy automatically becomes Bar Mitzvah at 13, it is traditional to mark the occasion in the synagogue on the Shabbat following his birthday. At the morning service he will be called up to the bimah to read his portion of the Torah. This can be very nerve-wracking because the synagogue is likely to be packed with family and friends who have come to witness this most important day in his life, as well as the usual Saturday congregation.

Many families hold a large party that Saturday evening or on the Sunday, so that everyone who has watched and helped the boy grow into manhood can celebrate the happy event. He will usually receive lots of cards and presents; a yad, a prayer book and a tallit are popular gifts on this occasion.

A girl comes of age

Orthodox Jewish girls do not have such a large celebration as the boys because they do not have the same religious obligations. Girls are believed to mature earlier than boys and so take on their personal religious responsibilities at 12. This can be marked by a smaller ceremony with a group of girls in the synagogue hall sometime after they have reached the required age. This is called Bat Chayil: *Bat* means 'daughter' and *chayil* means 'worth'. At this ceremony the girls may be asked to give a short presentation of some of the things they have learned in their year of study. This might include welcoming in Shabbat, keeping a kosher kitchen, or preparing for festivals in the home. A girl may be asked to talk about a study she has made of a famous Jewish woman in history. A girl's Bat Chayil can be followed by a small party. In Reform Judaism when a girl is 12, she can celebrate a Bat Mitzvah in exactly the same way as a boy.

1 What ceremony takes place when a boy is 13 years old?
2 Why is this an important day in his religious life?
3 What ceremony can mark an Orthodox girl taking on her religious duties?
4 What religious duties will a boy have after the age of 13?
5 List the ways in which a boy has to prepare for his Bar Mitzvah ceremony.

Topic 3 — Marriage

What is ...?

A Jewish couple marry under a canopy called a **huppah**. It symbolises harmony, and the home the couple will make together.

The bridegroom gives the bride a sip of wine as part of the ceremony.

Jews believe that it is God's plan for everyone to marry and have children, enabling people to take part in his work of creation. The first command in the Torah, made to Adam and Eve, was: '*Have many children so that your descendants will live all over the earth and bring it under their control.*' (Genesis 1:28) Jews take this seriously and believe that a married relationship is the best environment for bringing up children. Because it would be difficult for a non-Jew to follow the many religious rules, Jews believe they should marry another Jewish person. Orthodox Jews also believe that you can only be Jewish if you have a Jewish mother.

The marriage ceremony can take place anywhere, even out of doors. What is necessary is that the ceremony takes place under a huppah, which is a canopy. In its simplest form the huppah can be a tallit held over the couple. Many synagogues, however, set up an elaborate fringed huppah supported

What do you think?

'It is important for a Jew to marry another Jew.' Why would someone say that? Can you see any problems if a Jew does not marry another Jew?

by poles and decorated with flowers. The huppah symbolises the home the couple will make together. It is open on four sides to show that family and friends will always be welcome. The bride can wear whatever she wishes but traditionally chooses white as a sign of purity. The groom wears his tallit and has his head covered as a sign of respect for God.

The groom enters with his father and stands under the huppah waiting for the bride to enter. She comes in with both her parents and stands next to him. The rabbi takes the ceremony and begins by saying a blessing over a goblet of wine, to thank God for the marriage. This is handed to the groom, and he and his bride in turn each take a sip. The groom places a ring on the bride's finger saying: *'Behold you are consecrated to me by this ring, according to the Law of Moses and of Israel.'* These are the most important words in the ceremony; the couple are now married. In a Reform wedding ceremony, the bride can give the groom a ring and repeat the same words. The circular shape of the ring indicates that marriage is never-ending; it is for life. The ring is also a symbolic link with the chain of Jewish families going back to Abraham, to which this new family hope to add another generation.

After this the ketubah, the marriage contract, is read out. Here the husband states his intention to love and care for his wife and to provide for her in the event of divorce. A ketubah is traditionally written and read in Aramaic (a dialect of Hebrew) and signed by the husband. The marriage is sealed when the ketubah is handed to the bride.

Seven blessings are sung by the chazan, and the ceremony ends with a wine-glass being stamped upon by the groom. This dramatic gesture is said to symbolise that all marriages will have their good and bad times. Others say it is a reminder of the destruction of the Temple in Jerusalem. As the glass shatters, everyone shouts, *'Mazel Tov!'* which is Hebrew for 'Good luck!'

What is ...?

The **ketubah** is the marriage contract which is signed by the groom and given to his new wife. It states his intention to feed, clothe and care for her.

Questions

1 What is a huppah and what does it symbolise?
2 Why does the ring have an important part in the marriage ceremony?
3 Explain the importance of the ketubah in the ceremony.
4 Why is marriage and family life important in Judaism?
5 Give an account of the religious customs in a Jewish marriage ceremony.

Topic 4

Death and mourning

What is...?

Kaddish is the mourning prayer recited at the graveside. It praises the name of God, showing that life carries on.

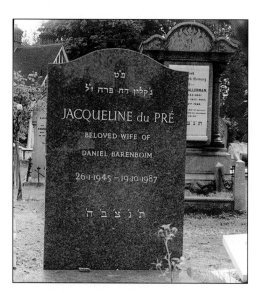

This is the grave of the famous cellist Jacqueline du Pré, who converted to Judaism. A visitor to her grave has placed a pebble on it.

Jews believe that death is simply a stage of existence and should not be feared. After death God will judge them, rewarding the good and punishing the evil. Judaism does not provide detailed teachings about the afterlife. As one prayer says: '*What can we know of death, we who cannot understand life?*'

A person who is dying is cared for. Someone will sit with them, help them to confess their sins and say the Shema, which every Jew hopes will be the last words they hear. The family can be helped by the chevra kaddisha, a group from the synagogue who volunteer to care for the dead and dying; men care for a man, women care for a woman.

After death the chevra kaddisha wash the body as a sign of spiritual cleanliness and prepare the person for burial. The body is wrapped in a plain white cloth, and the tallit can be put around the shoulders. The body is placed in a plain, simple coffin and someone stays with the deceased until the burial. Expensive funerals are thought wasteful because everyone is equal in death and the money is better given to the poor and needy.

Funerals are arranged quickly, within 24 hours if possible. The Torah says, '*You were made from soil, and you will become soil again*' (Genesis 3:19), which Orthodox Jews interpret as meaning a body must be buried not cremated. Reform Jews allow cremation. The coffin is taken directly to the funeral hall at the cemetery, where the rabbi takes the service. Prayers are said and close mourners rip the lapel of their clothes to show that their lives are torn by grief. The coffin is carried outside, and Psalm 91, praising God the protector, is recited as it is lowered into the grave. In Israel the body is wrapped in its shroud and lowered into the grave without a coffin, so fulfilling the scriptures by being in touch with the earth. The Kaddish

Funerals are held in a hall at the cemetery. After the service everyone goes out to the graveside for the burial.

prayer is read, praising God the Creator. Everyone present throws a shovelful of earth into the grave, symbolising their acceptance of this death. Words of comfort are said to the mourners, and everyone goes back to the hall to wash their hands, symbolising the separation of life from death.

Mourning

Close members of the family begin a seven-day period of deep mourning called shiva. They remain at home, cared for by friends who bring food and encourage them to talk about their loss. Mourners sit on low chairs and do nothing that involves pleasure or comfort. They do not shave, cut their hair, bathe, have sex, wear perfume or leather shoes, or change into fresh clothes. Instead they spend time grieving for their loved one. A Jahrzeit candle burns throughout the Shiva recalling the passage in Proverbs: '*A person's soul is the candle of the Lord*.' Once the seven days are over, mourners return to daily life but do not go to any entertainment in the 30 days following the funeral. A gravestone is erected six or twelve months after the burial, with a short ceremony at the grave to unveil it. The dead are not forgotten. The anniversary of the death is marked at home by lighting a Jahrzeit candle and reciting the Kaddish. Visitors to the grave traditionally place a stone, not flowers, upon it.

What is ...?

The first seven days of intense mourning are called **shiva**.

Questions

1 Who are the chevra kaddisha and what do they do?
2 Explain the religious customs that are followed at a Jewish funeral.
3 How are Jews remembered on the anniversary of their death?
4 'Jewish mourning customs are inconvenient and interfere with normal life. They do not help people who are mourning when a loved one has died.' Do you agree? Give reasons for your answer, showing that you have considered more than one point of view.

Do you understand...
the Jewish rites of passage?

Task 1

1 What is this ceremony called and when does it take place?
2 What is the name given to the man on the left, and what is his role?
3 Explain how this ceremony reminds Jews of the Covenant.

Task 2

Read this prayer, which is recited at a Bar Mitzvah.
1 Who will say this prayer? What is the evidence for this?

In the presence of my teachers, the leaders and the members of this holy congregation, I now prepare to take upon myself the duties which are binding on all the family of Israel. I ask their help in the years that lie ahead to strengthen my loyalty and devotion so that I may grow in charity and good deeds. I think also of those who have gone before me, who through all the troubles of the world preserved this heritage of holiness and goodness, so that I should enter into it now.

May I be a true Bar Mitzvah, taking my place in the community of Israel, accepting its responsibilities, rejoicing in its blessing. May I be a witness to the living God and His goodness, and the tradition that lives within me.

I remember all those who have helped me reach this time. I give thanks for the love and care of my family, the patience and instruction of my teachers, and the support and companionship of my friends.

In the Torah I have read the word of God. With your help may I go on to fulfil it in my life.

Amen.

2 The prayer mentions '*my teachers, the leaders and the members of this holy congregation*'. Who will be at the synagogue for this ceremony?
3 The prayer speaks of the '*instruction of my teachers*'. What sort of things will the boy have learned?
4 What are '*the duties*' this person will now have to fulfil?

Task 3

1 These are all objects used in a Jewish wedding ceremony. Explain how each is used and what it means.
2 'It is important to keep traditions going.' Would you agree? Show that you have considered more than one point of view in your answer.

Task 4

1 What is this candle called?
2 What other mourning customs are there?
3 Do you think that it is helpful for mourners to have a week off work, or school, to come to terms with the loss of a close relative? Or is it better to get straight back to normal life?

Task 5

How many of these Hebrew words can you define?
* shiva
* huppah
* Kaddish
* mohel
* Brit Milah
* Bat Chayil
* chevra kaddisha
* sandek

✓ Quick revision

* Baby boys are circumcised on the eighth day.
* Circumcision is a sign of the Jews' Covenant with God.
* Bar Mitzvah is when a 13-year-old boy takes on his religious responsibilities.
* Jews can marry anywhere, provided there is a huppah and two witnesses.
* Orthodox Jews do not allow cremation.

Topic 1 — Mezuzah

 **What is ...?**

A **mezuzah** is a parchment scroll containing the Shema prayer inside a case that is fixed to the right-hand side of a doorpost.

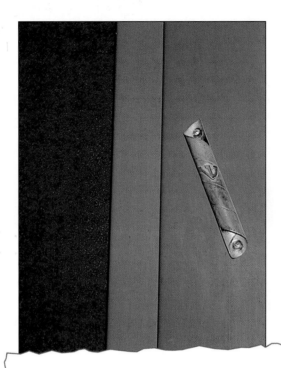

The mezuzah is usually fixed to the right-hand side of the doorpost, tilting into the room.

Hear O Israel, the Lord our God is one God. Love the Lord your God with all your heart, with all your soul, and with all your strength. Never forget these commands that I am giving you today. Teach them to your children. Repeat them when you are at home and when you are away, when you are resting and when you are working. Tie them on your arms and wear them on your foreheads as a reminder. Write them on the doorposts of your houses and on your gates.

(Deuteronomy 6:4–9)

To obey this mitzvah, or commandment, to write the words on their doorposts and gates, Jews write the words of the Shema on a parchment scroll and put that inside a case which they nail to the door-frame. The words are hand-written by a sofer with the same care he gives to writing a large Torah scroll. Although the mezuzah parchment is very small, it is prepared in the same way. The parchment must be from the skin of a kosher animal like a cow, sheep or goat, and the sofer prepares indelible ink from natural ingredients. He then writes the Hebrew using a quill pen. Traditionally the words of the Shema will fill 22 lines. The finished parchment is rolled up and tucked inside the mezuzah case.

The case can be made of any material that will protect the scroll: plastic, metal, glass and pottery are all used. An Orthodox Jew may have

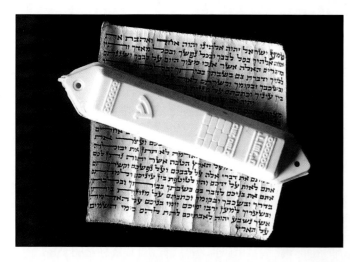

Inside a mezuzah is a hand-written piece of parchment with the Shema prayer on it.

a mezuzah fixed to every door inside the house (except the toilet and cupboards); Reform Jews usually just have a mezuzah on their front door. A Jewish person touches the mezuzah with their fingers as they pass, and some people will then put their fingers to their lips. By touching the mezuzah on entering and leaving a room, Jews are reminded of the presence of God. A very observant Jew might also recite line 5 from Psalm 121: *'The Lord will guard you; he is by your side to protect you.'*

A mezuzah fixed to the doorpost is a sign of a Jewish household. Nailing up the mezuzah is one of the first things a family does when they move into a new home. Many Jewish shops or offices also have a mezuzah on their doors to remind all who enter of the presence of God.

The mezuzah is:

- an outward sign of God's presence
- a reminder to Jews of God's protection
- a reminder to Jews that they have a duty to obey God's commandments
- an acknowledgement of the relationship between God and man.

Twice in seven years the mezuzah case must be opened and examined by the sofer to ensure that the scroll is still legible. If the writing is in places then a new mezuzah scroll will be put in the case.

What do you think?

Why do you think the use of the mezuzah is described as a discipline for Jews? Do you think it is helpful, or just an empty gesture?

Questions

1 What is a mezuzah?
2 Where would you expect to find a mezuzah?
3 What does a mezuzah symbolise?
4 Explain how Jews are obeying God's commandments by their use of the mezuzah.

Dietary laws

What is...?

Kosher means something that is good and proper according to Jewish law. It is usually used to describe food.

This establishment is under the supervision of the

KASHRUT DIVISION

LONDON BETH DIN

תחת השגחת בית דין צדק
דק״ק לונדון והמדינה

This Jewish baker has been inspected and licensed as a kosher food shop by the Bet Din (it can be spelt Bet or Beth).

In ancient times God gave the Jews detailed rules about the sort of food that was good and safe for them to eat. These are known as the laws of kashrut, or the kosher rules. Jews eat kosher food because it is commanded in the Torah, and they are showing obedience to God by following these rules.

Detailed rules about which animals, birds and fish are acceptable appear in Leviticus 11 in the Torah. Here is a summary:

Food is carefully labelled to help Jews ensure they eat food that is kosher. This label has a K for kosher and a D to show it is a dairy product (chocolate contains milk). The stamp shows it has been checked and approved by the Bet Din.

* *'You may eat any land animal that has divided hooves and that also chews the cud.'* This includes meat like lamb, beef, goat and most herbivores. The pig does have a divided hoof but it does not chew the cud, so all forms of pork or bacon are forbidden.

* *'You may eat any kind of fish that has fins and scales.'* This includes most fish but forbids other seafood like shellfish or creatures like eels.

* Birds that have been farmed, e.g. turkey, chicken and duck. This includes most poultry but not pheasants and other birds that are hunted.

CLUB Fruit combines thick milk chocolate with chewy fruit, chocolate flavoured cream and a crunchy biscuit

INGREDIENTS: Milk Chocolate (49%), Wheat Flour, Vegetable and Hydrogenated Vegetable Oil, Currants (8%), Glucose Syrup, Sugar, Fat Reduced Cocoa Powder, Emulsifier: Soya Lecithins, Raising Agents (Ammonium Bicarbonate, Sodium Bicarbonate, Disodium Diphosphate), Rolled Oats, Salt.

DANONE TM
A company of the DANONE GROUP

The Jacob's Bakery Limited, P.O. Box 14, Liverpool, L9 7JX, U.K. Made in England
All affixed Trademarks belong to, or are used under licence by, subsidiaries of the DANONE GROUP.

Suitable for Vegetarians

K D

5013 7961

Preparation

It also states several times in the Torah, '*The one thing you must not eat is meat with blood still in it; I forbid this because the life is in the blood.*' (Genesis 9:4) This rule affects the way Jews prepare their meat. Animals must be killed in a ritual manner called shechitah. Only a shochet, a licensed Jewish butcher trained in the kosher method of slaughter, is permitted to kill an animal. The animal's throat is cut swiftly with a sharp knife and without pre-stunning. This method is said to avoid cruelty because death is instantaneous.

The carcass is then hung up to drain away the blood. When the meat has been jointed, it is soaked in salted water to remove the blood, then rinsed before cooking.

The meat and milk rule

Three times in the Torah it says: '*Do not cook a young sheep or goat in its mother's milk.*' (Exodus 23:19) Jews believe that this means it is forbidden to use milk, which comes from a living animal, with meat, which comes from a dead animal. As a result the two products are never eaten within the same meal. If meat is to be cooked and eaten for dinner, then foods like yogurt or ice cream cannot be eaten as part of the sweet course. Cheese cannot be substituted either because it also contains milk, but a fruit course would be acceptable.

Orthodox Jews take great care to ensure there is no accidental mixing of meat and milk in the preparation of food. They have two separate areas in the kitchen, one for the preparation and washing-up of meat dishes and the other for milk dishes. There is one sink, cupboards and utensils (with red handles) for meat products, and another set (with blue handles) for using with milk products. Reform Jews vary in how strictly they keep the kosher rules. Some may eat kosher food but do not necessarily have a separated kitchen. Most Jews would argue that family life is at the heart of their religion.

What is...?

A **shochet** is a Jewish butcher who is trained in the kosher method of slaughter called **shechitah**.

Activity

Plan a kosher meal for an Orthodox Jew. A useful tip is to decide at the outset whether you are going to serve a meat or a vegetarian main course.

Questions

1 What does the word 'kosher' mean?
2 Why does Jewish food have to be kosher?
3 State two ways in which the Jewish dietary rules affect the preparation of food.
4 'It is very difficult for a Jew to eat kosher in Britain today.' Do you agree? Show that you have considered both sides of the issue.

Topic 3

Family life

What is ...?

The **family** is important in Judaism because it is the place where the religion is learned and passed on.

The family is seen as the heart of Jewish life.

Without Jewish families the religion would simply disappear and no amount of synagogue attendance or Torah reading could prevent that. Judaism is transmitted through the family. For Orthodox Jews to be Jewish they must have a Jewish mother; some Reform groups accept a person as Jewish if either parent was a Jew. Not only is the religion a matter of inheritance but home is the place where Jewish customs are learned. Most festivals are celebrated in the home, and children frequently have their own special part in the ceremony, so they learn the historical story and its meaning along with the ritual. The rules of kosher, the dietary laws, are practised in the home, so a young person grows up understanding how to keep these rules, and about their importance. The mezuzah fixed to the front door is an outward sign that God has a place in this home. Within the Jewish family everyone has a part to play to ensure the smooth running and harmony of Jewish society.

What do you think?

In answer to a question about finding God, one learned rabbi said. 'If you are looking for God, go home!' What do you think he meant by that?

Children's responsibilities

The Torah says that children have a duty towards their parents. The fifth of the Ten Commandments states: '*Respect your father and your mother, so that you may live a long time in the land that I am giving you.*' (Exodus 20:12) There are many other reminders of a child's duty in the scriptures. The book of Proverbs says: '*Make your father and mother proud of you; give your mother that happiness.*' (Proverbs 23:25) Everybody is a child of somebody, and Jews believe the responsibility to respect your parents does not end when you become Bar Mitzvah or Bat Chayil. Jews are told to: '*Listen to your father; without him you would not exist. When your mother is old, show her your appreciation.*' (Proverbs 23:22) The Talmud also instructs Jews to look after their parents even though they are elderly: '*See that they eat and drink and take them where they need to go.*' This means that every family has a duty to ensure the grandparents are well provided for. If they do not live with the family, it is still the family's responsibility to ensure they are cared for in a residential home that caters for their needs, for example their kosher diet.

Parents' responsibilities

Responsibility is a two-way thing in Judaism. Just as children have a duty towards their parents, so parents have a duty to their children. One of the most important things a parent can do for their child is to educate it. A mother is chiefly responsible for teaching her children the rituals and traditions of Judaism in the home. They watch her prepare for Shabbat, then open the weekly festival by lighting two candles and saying a blessing over them. By setting a good example a mother is expected to strengthen the family's religious life and commitment. The father also has a responsibility for setting a good example to his children, and in addition he is required to teach them how to lead useful lives of their own. The Talmud carries a stark warning to fathers: '*He who does not teach his son a trade is as though he taught him to be a robber.*' One of the early rabbis even insisted that a father had a duty to teach his son to swim. The idea behind it is that you owe it to your children to teach them essential survival skills.

The importance placed on parents teaching their children is set out in the Shema: '*Never forget these commands that I am giving you today. Teach them to your children.*' (Deuteronomy 6:6–7)

Questions

1 How should Jewish children treat their parents?
2 What duties do the parents have towards their children?
3 Explain why family life is important in Judaism.
4 'Home, not the synagogue, is the centre of Judaism.' Do you agree with this statement? Give reasons for your answer, showing that you have considered more than one point of view.

Topic 4

Relationships

6: Home life

KOSHER SEX

A RECIPE FOR PASSION AND INTIMACY

SHMULEY BOTEACH

Author of *Dating Secrets of the Ten Commandments*

Sex is seen as an essential part of Jewish married life.

Judaism has always accepted that sex is a natural and pleasurable activity. Jews believe there is no virtue in remaining celibate (that means living a life without sex). However, sex should only take place within marriage where it will deepen the relationship between a husband and wife. The seventh of the Ten Commandments states: '*Do not commit adultery*.' (Exodus 20:14) In biblical times the penalty for adultery was death for both guilty people. Whilst this is not the penalty today, adultery is nevertheless strictly forbidden. Living together is not acceptable to Orthodox Jews. Any children born to an unmarried couple are illegitimate and will only be allowed to marry another illegitimate Jew or a convert to Judaism. In order to avoid young people being tempted into sexual relationships before marriage, Orthodox Jews educate their children in single-sex schools, and the sexes sit apart in the synagogue.

All Jews are encouraged to marry. Sex within marriage is seen as a husband's duty and a wife's right, and it is encouraged for pleasure as well as the creation of children. It is said to be a particular blessing if a couple make love on Shabbat. Obeying the command in the Torah, '*Do not have intercourse with a woman during her monthly period, because she is ritually unclean*' (Leviticus 18:19), a Jewish couple abstain from sex during this time. Blood is regarded as an impurity, and a week following her period a wife must be ritually cleansed. She goes to a mikveh, a special immersion bath-house run by the local Jewish community.

What is ...?

A **mikveh** is a ritual bath which a wife takes after her period before she can resume sexual relations with her husband.

70

After removing all her clothes, jewellery and make-up, she showers, then goes completely under the water in the bath. After this ceremonial cleansing the couple are able to resume sexual relations. Jews believe this time of sexual abstinence strengthens the couple's love for each other.

Orthodox Jews believe that a homosexual relationship is wrong because the Torah states: '*No man is to have sexual relations with another man; God hates that.*' (Leviticus 18:22) If someone is gay, Jews believe they should control their inclinations and lead a celibate life. Homosexual behaviour, they believe, may have terrible consequences, like the transmission of AIDS. Reform Judaism, however, accepts that some people may be happiest in a gay relationship. All Jews, Orthodox or Reform, should show tolerance towards homosexuals and not persecute them, because they are all part of God's creation. Jews are expected to show compassion to a person suffering from HIV or AIDS and give them as much help and support as possible.

Divorce

It is accepted that, despite everyone's best efforts, some marriages do not work out. Divorce is permitted in Judaism although it is considered a very sad thing: the Talmud says, '*even the altar sheds tears*'. If a couple agree that their marriage can no longer continue, the husband goes to the Bet Din to request a get – that is, a certificate of divorce. No reasons are required for a divorce and no blame is attached to either person. The wife presents herself to the Bet Din to hand back her marriage ketubah (see page 59) and receives a get from her husband. It says:

What is ...?

A Jewish certificate of divorce is called a **get**. It is issued by the Bet Din.

> Thus do I set you free, I release you, and put aside, in order that you may have permission and authority over yourself to go and marry any man you may desire. No person may hinder you from this day onward, and you are permitted to every man. This shall be for you from me a bill of dismissal, a letter of release, and a document of freedom, in accordance with the laws of Moses and of Israel.

In most countries it is also necessary for the couple to obtain a civil divorce through the courts for the marriage to be at a legal end. A person who has been divorced has no slur on their name and is encouraged to marry again in the synagogue.

Questions

1 What is the Jewish attitude towards a couple living together?
2 Is divorce allowed in Judaism?
3 How do Orthodox and Reform Judaism differ in their attitude towards gay relationships?
4 Why does a woman have to go to the mikveh once a month?
5 'Married couples are the only people who should have sex.' Consider the arguments for and against this statement, taking care to explain how an Orthodox Jew would respond.

Do you understand...

Jewish home life?

'You will be blessed when you come in, you will be blessed when you go out.'

Task 1

1 a What is this called?
   b Where would you expect to see one?
2 What is inside this case?
3 Why do Jews have one?
4 What might a Jew do as they walk past it, and why?

Task 2

1 What does the letter K on this label mean?
2 Why do Jews pay great attention to the labels on the food that they eat?
3 What fish would be acceptable to a Jewish person?
4 Explain how these words from the Torah will affect the way a Jew prepares their food: *'The life of every living thing is in the blood, and that is why the Lord has told the people of Israel that they shall not eat any meat with blood still in it.'* (Leviticus 17:14)

 INGREDIENTS
Wheat Flour, Vegetable and Hydrogenated Vegetable Oil, Salt, Raising Agent (Sodium Bicarbonate), Yeast.

 K $^{L}_{B}$$_{D}$ Suitable for Vegetarians

Task 3

1 Why don't Jews eat meat and milk in the same meal?
2 How would an Orthodox Jew design their kitchen?
3 'Believing in God is what matters, not following lots of rules and rituals.'
   Do you agree? Give reasons for your answer, and show that you have
   considered more than one point of view.

Task 4

JEWISH LESBIAN & GAY COMMUNITY

BM – JGLG
LONDON
WCIN 3XX

Tel: 020 8922 5214

www.jglg.org.uk
E mail: secretary@jglg.org.uk

1 What is the Orthodox Jewish attitude towards homosexual relationships,
   and why?
2 What sort of relationship do Orthodox Jews think is the correct one
   for a sexual relationship?
3 Explain how a Jew can get divorced.
4 'Having a strong religion within the family helps young people to have high
   moral standards in their own life.' Do you agree? Give reasons for your
   answer, showing that you have considered more than one point of view.

Task 5

How many of these Hebrew words can you define?
*   mikveh
*   mezuzah
*   kashrut
*   kosher
*   shochet
*   get
*   shechitah

✓ Quick revision

*   The Bet Din grants a divorce and gives the woman a get.
*   Sexual relations are only acceptable within marriage.
*   Family life is at the heart of Judaism.
*   The mezuzah case contains the Shema.

Topic 1

Justice and the law

 Activity

Read this piece from the Torah:

> Appoint judges and other officials in every town that the Lord your God gives you. These men are to judge the people impartially. They are not to be unjust or show partiality in their judgements; and they are not to accept bribes, for gifts blind the eyes ... and cause them to give wrong decisions. Always be fair and just, so that you will occupy the land that the Lord your God is giving you and will continue to live there.
>
> (Deuteronomy 16:18–20)

List the advice given here for officials. Do you think it has any relevance for today?

 What is ...?

The **Halakhah** is the name given to the Jewish law which is based on the Torah.

Jews believe that God gave people the laws for living when he gave Moses the Torah on Mount Sinai. It is for this reason that the word 'Torah' means the law. These first five books of the Tenakh contain everything Jews need to know about how they should behave. The law code that has been drawn up from this by the rabbis over the centuries is called the Halakhah. It covers all aspects of life, from the rules for religious observance to criminal and civil law. Israel is the only country where Jews live under Jewish laws. In other countries they must abide by the laws of the land, but in those countries the Halakhah is overseen by the Bet Din, the special Jewish court of three rabbis (see page 33). Matters that usually occupy the Bet Din are religious issues like the dietary rules, Jewish divorce and conversion to Judaism. If, however, two Jews have a civil dispute over a personal or business matter, they can take their case to the Bet Din for judgement according to the Halakhah, rather than go to a civil court.

 What do you think?

Do you think requiring two independent witnesses to a murder before carrying out the death penalty could prevent the wrong person from being executed?

Jews believe that if everyone were to take notice of the advice in the Torah to *'love your neighbour as you love yourself'* (Leviticus 19:18), everything would be well. People have been given free-will by God and some choose not to obey the rules set by God. The Torah says that people who break the rules must be held responsible for their actions. By punishing people for doing wrong, Jews believe it not only makes them pay for their crime but acts as a deterrent to others.

The Ten Commandments were a code of conduct set up over 3,000 years ago. Some rules remain the same today.

The Ten Commandments

1. Do not worship any other god but me.
2. Do not worship idols.
3. Do not use the name of God without reason.
4. Keep the Sabbath holy.
5. Respect your father and mother.
6. Do not murder.
7. Do not commit adultery.
8. Do not steal.
9. Do not tell lies.
10. Do not envy other people's property.

The death penalty

The ultimate punishment for some crimes is death, and the Torah names various crimes that warrant execution by hanging or stoning: *'Anyone who commits murder shall be put to death... The principle is a life for a life.'* (Leviticus 24:17–18) Although this was stated in the Torah, it was a punishment that could only be used in extreme cases. A murderer could only be executed if there were two independent witnesses to the crime and if the murderer fully understood the consequences of his action. If this was the case, the execution had to be carried out as swiftly and humanely as possible, with no mutilation of the body during the execution. Modern Israel abolished the death penalty in the 1950s for everything except treason or genocide, and has only executed one person in its history.

Since its creation in 1948, Israel has only executed one person. Adolf Eichmann, a leading Nazi, was found guilty of the murder of thousands of Jews during the Holocaust. He was executed in 1963.

Questions

1 What is the Halakhah based on?
2 Who oversees the keeping of the Halakhah in Britain?
3 Do Jews believe in the death penalty?
4 'It is only right to kill a murderer.' Do you agree? What would a Jewish person think about this statement?

Topic 2

Racism and prejudice

What is ...?

Anti-semitism is the term given to persecution that is targeted at Jews.

What is ...?

The **pogroms** were racial attacks on the Jews in Russia.

The **Holocaust** was a racial attack by the Nazis which killed 6 million Jews.

What is ...?

Racism is a particular form of prejudice. It is when someone is picked on because they are a different nationality or colour.

Jews can still find themselves the victims of prejudice. This is called anti-semitism when they are the butt of jokes about their traditions or their clothing. In more extreme cases Jewish graves are vandalised, kosher shops and synagogues attacked, even Jews themselves beaten up in the street. Fortunately such cases are rare in Britain.

What do you think?

Do you think it is worth encouraging people to treat others as they would like to be treated themselves? Or is this an unrealistic aim?

Prejudice is not something that only happens to Jews. All sorts of people suffer from prejudice – the old, the disabled, gay people, coloured people – absolutely anyone can find themselves picked being on because they are in some way 'different' from the rest. Disliking someone and being biased against them is prejudice. At its worst prejudice can develop into persecution which is hatred, continual harassment and violence. It can be directed against one person or a whole group of people. When it involves hatred of a whole race it is called racism. Jews believe it is wrong to be racist because everyone was created by God and is valued by God. To discriminate against a person on account of their race is to deny that they are God's creation.

Jews believe all forms of prejudice are wrong. It says in the Torah: '*God created human beings, making them to be like himself.*' (Genesis 1:27) So if people are made by God, and like God, it would be wrong to hate them. It is also believed that everyone has been created to play their part in God's great plan for mankind and to serve God in different ways. Although Jews believe themselves to be the chosen people, they should be tolerant of other religions, accepting that there may be different ways of serving God.

For thousands of years the Jews have been picked on and mistreated simply because they were Jews. Apart from the ancient stories of their slavery in Egypt, there have been many times in the past millennium when the Jews were persecuted in Russia and Germany. They got the blame for things that were going wrong in the country and became scapegoats. Jews were easily picked out on account of their traditions or their facial features, and they were made the butt of jokes and then vicious attacks. English literature has many examples of prejudice against Jews, from Shylock in Shakespeare's *Merchant of Venice* to Fagin in Dickens' novel *Oliver Twist*.

Having been the victims of persecution themselves, Jews have a strong belief that it is wrong to mistreat anyone who is different. The Torah tells them: '*Do not ill-treat foreigners who are living in your land. Treat them as you would a fellow-Israelite, and love them as you love yourselves. Remember that you were once a foreigner in the land of Egypt.*' (Leviticus 19:33–34)

Questions

1 What does the word 'prejudice' mean?
2 Explain Jewish beliefs about racial and religious discrimination.
3 Explain some of the ways in which Jews have been the victims of persecution in the past.
4 'Prejudice is not a serious problem today.' Do you agree? Give reasons for your answers, showing that you have considered more than one point of view.

Topic 3

Role and status of women

Does this woman belong to the Orthodox or Reform tradition? How can you tell?

Motherhood is seen as a great responsibility in Judaism, but women are not forbidden to go out to work.

 What do you think?

'The sexes are biologically different, so equality in daily life is an impossibility.' Do you agree with this view? Explain your answer.

A woman has an important part to play in Jewish life, which is of equal value to a man's but is different. Because the man's role is seen in public and the woman's takes place in the home, many people who are not Jewish say the religion is sexist. Indeed, some people who are Jewish believe that the role of women in the religion needs to change as society changes. The result is that in Reform Judaism women can perform similar religious duties to men.

It has always been accepted that a married woman in Judaism is likely to have the responsibility of motherhood. This is important because she will be the person who passes on Judaism to her children. In Orthodox Judaism a person can only be Jewish if they have a Jewish mother. Equally the mother is the person responsible for teaching her children how to live a Jewish life. It is in the home that most of us learn how to behave towards others and what is right and what is wrong. In a Jewish household children learn about prayer, and what is kosher, as well as all the traditions and rituals associated with festivals.

Because it is not easy to fit in set prayer times with the feeding times of a small baby, Jewish women were never given the same religious obligations as men. A Jewish man is required to pray three times a day, in the morning, afternoon and evening. A woman only needs to pray twice a day, in the morning and afternoon. Some women see this as freedom to devote themselves to their children, whilst others interpret it as a sign they have not been given the same religious status as men.

In Orthodox Judaism women are not required to take part in congregational prayer and so they cannot be counted as one of the minyan (see page 29). In the synagogue they sit apart from the men, usually in a gallery or an area at the back. This is so that neither sex will distract the other from worship. When an Orthodox woman attends synagogue she does not have an active role. She remains upstairs throughout the service and is not permitted to touch the Torah, nor read from it, nor lead any of the prayers.

In Reform Judaism a woman can hold any of the synagogue offices, from rabbi or chazan to treasurer. She is allowed to wear a tallit for morning prayer if she wishes and could be counted part of the minyan, although many Reform synagogues do not require a minyan to be present for worship to take place. Families often sit together in the synagogue, so men and women can sit side by side if they wish. A 12-year-old girl can celebrate her Bat Mitzvah in the Reform synagogue in the same way as a boy would celebrate his Bar Mitzvah.

In the home there is less distinction between Orthodox and Reform women. Most would teach their children about their faith, welcome in Shabbat and make the traditional preparations for festivals. All Jewish mothers try to set a good example to their children and support the family's religious life. Because of her important role in family life, the Jewish mother is respected in both traditions.

Questions

1 **a** What prayer obligations do women have?
  b Why are these different from those of the men?
2 Name two ways in which Reform Jews have changed the role of women in synagogue worship.
3 Describe the importance of a Jewish mother in an Orthodox family.
4 'Men and women are of equal importance in Judaism.' Do you agree? Show that you have considered some of the different views that might be expressed.

Topic 4 Wealth and poverty

The fact that some people have lots of money and some barely have enough to survive has perplexed people throughout history. The Torah was realistic, saying: *'There will always be some Israelites who are poor and in need, and so I command you to be generous to them.'* (Deuteronomy 15:11) Jews believe that God decides who is to be rich and who is to be poor – neither situation is a disgrace. It is quite acceptable to be rich. *'If God gives a man wealth and property and lets him enjoy them, he should be grateful and enjoy what he has worked for. It is a gift from God.'* (Ecclesiastes 5:19) What is considered wrong is for someone to be so obsessed by money that they spend all their time trying to make more. *'We leave this world just as we entered it – with nothing. In spite of all our work there is nothing we can take with us.'* (Ecclesiastes 5:15) Everyone has a duty to help the poor. Nobody enjoys being poor; as the Talmud says: *'Poverty is worse than 50 plagues.'* At festival times especially, money should be given so that the poor can enjoy the celebrations too.

The Hebrew scriptures contain practical advice about how the poor can be fed. At harvest farmers should leave corn growing at the edges of their fields for the poor to collect. Fruits like grapes and olives that were missed during the first picking should be left for the poor to gather. Every seventh year when a field is left fallow, poor people and wildlife can take what grows. Details are also given of a Jubilee Year:

At the end of every seventh year you are to cancel the debts of those who owe you money. This is how it is to be done. All who have lent money to a fellow-Israelite are to cancel the debt; he must not try to collect the money; the Lord himself has declared the debt cancelled.

(Deuteronomy 15:1–2)

Jews were instructed that any slaves they owned must be given their freedom after they had served their master for six years. A freed slave was also to be provided with the basic necessities.

> Give to them generously from what the Lord has blessed you with – sheep, corn and wine. Remember that you were slaves in Egypt and the Lord your God set you free; that is why I am giving you this command.
>
> (Deuteronomy 15:14–15)

All these ways of helping the less well-off were simply considered a fair and just thing to do, rather than a gesture of overwhelming generosity.

There are two main ways in which all Jews today should care for the less well-off:

1 Tzedaka

The scriptures say that everyone should give a tenth of their income to the poor. Even someone receiving charity is expected to give that proportion to a poorer person. The word tzedaka literally means 'justice'. Jews do not believe they are 'being good' by paying tzedaka, it is a fair thing to do. When giving and receiving charity, particular attention must be paid to preserving someone's dignity. Nobody likes accepting charity, so Jews try to make it easier for all concerned by encouraging tzedaka to be paid to an organised charity. Then a poor person can receive their rightful share without the embarrassment of knowing exactly who gave the money.

2 Gemilat chassadim

Everyone can do a good deed to someone else. It may be a spontaneous donation to a good cause or not involve money at all. Taking time to help or say a kind word is a form of charity.

What is...?

The word **tzedaka** is the Hebrew word for charity. A Jew should donate 10 per cent of their income to the poor.

These two Jewish girls are working for the Jewish charity Tzedek. They volunteered to give up eight weeks to help set up a youth club in Zimbabwe, and each had to raise £1,250 to pay their expenses. The charity works in Africa and India, helping anyone in need.

Questions

1 Do Jews think it is wrong to have a lot of money?
2 Is a poor person obliged to do anything for charity?
3 Explain the Jewish attitude towards wealth and poverty in the world.
4 'One-tenth of all the produce of the land, whether grain or fruit, belongs to the Lord.' How would a modern Jew put this quotation from Leviticus into operation?

Topic 5

Peace and war

Modern Israel has been involved in several conflicts since its foundation.
Most, it is argued, have been in defence of its territories.

Peace

Judaism believes that peace is the ideal and will be achieved in the future.
There will come a time of peace on earth for all living creatures, called the
Messianic Age (see page 15). The prophet Isaiah spoke of it as a time when
*'They will hammer their swords into ploughs and their spears into pruning-
knives. Nation will never again go to war, never prepare for battle again.'*
(Isaiah 2:4)

The prophet Micah said: *'Everyone will live in peace among his own
vineyards and fig trees, and no one will make him afraid. The Lord
Almighty has promised this.'* (Micah 4:4)

The Jewish belief in peace is shown by their standard greeting, 'Shalom!'
which means 'Peace!' It is used in the same way as people say 'Hallo' when

 What do you think?

'More wars have been fought over religion than anything else.' Do
you agree? How do you think a Jew would respond to this statement?

they meet. Whilst it is thought that peace is desirable, it is agreed that it is hard to achieve in an imperfect world.

War

Jews are not pacifists. They believe that war is an acceptable last resort when discussions have failed. All able-bodied men were expected to serve in the army in biblical times, with the exception of the priests and newly-weds. Jews' suffering throughout history, notably when 6 million Jews died in the Holocaust, has taught them the need for self-defence and opposition to evil.

Jews believe that two types of war are permissible:

- An obligatory war, called milchemet mitzvah in Hebrew. This is a war commanded by God, like the occasions in the past when God ordered Jewish leaders into battle to gain the Promised Land. A war of self-defence is also considered an obligatory war.

- An optional war is called milchemet reshut in Hebrew. This would be permitted if you were going to be attacked and fought to prevent it. The Talmud says, '*If someone comes to kill you, kill him first.*' A war fought to defend another country and prevent war spreading belongs in this category.

Strict rules were laid down in the Torah about waging wars to prevent them developing into vendettas which were endless and destructive. Exodus 21:23–25 states: '*The punishment shall be life for life, eye for eye, tooth for tooth, hand for hand, foot for foot, burn for burn, wound for wound, bruise for bruise.*' This means revenge is to be limited to exactly the same wrong. Jews are forbidden to go to war to extend their territory.

The conduct of a war was strictly controlled. Deuteronomy 20:10 required the Jews to show mercy wherever possible: '*When you go to attack a city, first give its people a chance to surrender.*' In the book of Proverbs (25:21–22) the Jews were told: '*If your enemies are hungry, feed them; if they are thirsty, give them a drink. You will make them burn with shame, and the Lord will reward you.*' Jewish soldiers were forbidden to go on a spree of wanton destruction. Equally the innocent bystanders in a war, like the women, were to be treated with respect.

Jews today accept the view that nuclear weapons are a major threat to the human race but believe they serve a purpose. They keep the peace. It is argued that since the Second World War there have been no world wars, nor lives lost, because of nuclear weapons, whereas millions of people have been killed by conventional weapons.

Obligatory war is one that has been commanded by God.

Optional war is a war started to prevent a greater calamity.

Questions

1 Do you think Jews welcome the chance to go to war?
2 What would be an acceptable reason for a Jew to go to war?
3 What is the difference between an obligatory war and an optional war?
4 'Wars breed wars. Pacifism is the only answer.' What do you think? How would a Jew respond?

Topic 6

Holocaust

This heap of shoes came from Jews who went to the gas chambers at Auschwitz-Birkenau. Each pair of shoes was one person.

What is ...?

The worst massacre of Jews in modern times is called the **Holocaust**. Between 1933 and 1945, Hitler arranged the murder of 6 million Jews – one-third of the world's Jews.

The Jews have been the victims of many persecutions throughout history but by far the worst was the Holocaust. Between 1933 and 1945, Hitler and the Nazi Party in Germany arranged the systematic annihilation of Jews in Europe. Hitler was looking for people to blame for the Germans' shameful defeat in the First World War. He picked on the Jews as the scapegoats. In the beginning German Jews had their rights taken away; they could not own businesses, travel around freely or use public facilities like swimming baths or libraries. Later they were harassed and beaten up on the street, and their synagogues were burnt down. The situation worsened. Whole families were rounded up and sent to concentration camps where many were gassed, worked to death or suffered the most appalling atrocities. As the German war-machine over-ran neighbouring countries, even more Jews suffered the same fate. By the end of the Second World War, one-third of the entire Jewish population in the world was dead. Judaism in Eastern Europe had been virtually wiped out.

Activity

Look at the website www.vhf.org, which is the site of the Survivors of the Shoah Visual History Foundation. It was set up by Stephen Spielberg after the making of the film *Schindler's List* to record memories of survivors. Or you could look at www.bethshalom.com, a British Holocaust Memorial Centre.

One of the positive outcomes of the Holocaust was the creation of the modern state of Israel. In 1948, after the Second World War, the Jews were given their own country in the hope that they would never again suffer such persecution. Because most of those who died in the concentration camps had no grave, Israel created a permanent memorial to them (see page 11). Just outside Jerusalem is Yad Vashem, the Holocaust Memorial Park. At its heart is the Hall of Remembrance where the names of the 22 death camps are inscribed on the floor and an eternal flame is kept burning. The one and a half million babies and children who were murdered have their own memorial at Yad Vashem. As visitors walk through their memorial room, which though dark is lit with a flickering candle spark for each child, the names of the children are recited. Modern sculptures in the grounds of Yad Vashem commemorate many different aspects of the Holocaust.

This is one of the many modern monuments at Yad Vashem which commemorate the lives of the 6 million Jews killed in the Holocaust.

One day a year is set aside in the Jewish calendar to remember those who died in the Holocaust, because virtually every Jewish family lost relatives. The day is called Yom Hashoah, or Holocaust Day. This is a very solemn day, when all shops and entertainment are closed in Israel. Some Jews attend synagogue services or pray at home, others light a Jahrzeit candle in memory of those who died.

In Britain an annual Holocaust Remembrance Day was set up on 27 January 2000 to commemorate all the Jews who lost their lives at the hands of the Nazis. In the same year the Imperial War Museum in London created a permanent Holocaust Exhibition, and plans for a National Holocaust Museum in Manchester were finalised.

Jews believe it is vital that the Holocaust is not forgotten. By keeping alive the memory of the 6 million who died, Jews show they have prevented Hitler from eradicating them forever. They also argue that such horrendous actions must never be forgotten, or they might happen again.

Questions

1 What was the Holocaust?
2 Why should Jews remember it today?
3 Explain the ways in which Jews remember Jewish victims of the Holocaust.
4 'I think we should forget about the Holocaust. It all happened a long time ago and it just upsets people to think about it.'
   What do *you* think? Give reasons for your answer, showing that you have considered more than one point of view.

Do you understand...

Jewish beliefs about justice and equality?

Task 1

Women have to do compulsory military service in Israel, like the men.

1 What is the Jewish attitude towards peace?
2 State two reasons why a Jew might be prepared to go to war.
3 What is the Jewish teaching on capital punishment?

Task 2

Tzedek is a Jewish overseas development charity set up in 1990. One of its aims is 'to provide direct support to the developing world, working towards the relief and elimination of poverty regardless of race or religion'.

1 What is tzedaka?
2 Why do Jews think some people are rich and some are poor?
3 How do the aims of Tzedek fit with the Torah's teachings about charity and prejudice?
4 'Expecting a poor person to give a tenth of the charity they have just received is silly.' What would an Orthodox Jew say to this? What is your opinion?

Task 3

This Holocaust memorial is at Bet Shalom, a British Holocaust Centre. The six branches on the arms represent the 6 million victims of the Holocaust. The statue also looks like the menorah.

1 What was the Holocaust?
2 Why do Jews think it should never be forgotten?
3 State two ways in which Holocaust victims are remembered.

Task 4

How many of these words can you define?

- anti-semitism
- pogrom
- Halakhah
- racism
- Holocaust
- tzedaka

Quick revision

- Jews are commanded to treat all races equally.
- Yom Hashoah is the Holocaust Day.
- Jews should give one-tenth of their income to charity.
- The Holocaust killed 6 million Jews.

Topic 1

Created world

Jews outside Israel often sponsor tree-planting in their homeland.

In the book of Genesis it says that God created this planet and everything on it – plants, animals and people. As the earth's creator, God is also its owner; humans do not own the earth but they were told by God, '*Be glad and rejoice for ever in what I create*.' (Isaiah 65:18) This is taken to mean that people can enjoy God's creation to satisfy their needs: plants can be eaten, or used to make things, and animals can be eaten or used to work for humans.

The Torah contains much specific advice about how people should use God's created world for their needs, such as the following passage:

> *When you are trying to capture a city, do not cut down its fruit trees, even though the siege lasts a long time. Eat the fruit, but do not destroy the trees; the trees are not your enemies.*
>
> (Deuteronomy 20:19)

Rabbis have interpreted this to mean that wanton destruction of the environment is wrong. The 'scorched earth policy' of destroying villages, killing farm animals and setting fire to crops operated by some armies before they leave a region is totally against Judaism. Dumping waste chemicals in the sea which harm marine life would also be wrong.

Jews believe that people are stewards of God's world. Whilst they are on God's earth they can use its resources but they must hand everything on to the next generation in good condition. This encourages a 'green' approach to living, with emphasis on conserving the environment and recycling things rather than dumping them. Jews accept the need to cut trees down for building materials but these must be replaced. In Israel the people celebrate a spring festival called Tu B'Shevat, when children plant saplings. This is a sign of respect for God's creation as well as a practical way of replenishing the land. Jews around the world often send money to Israel to sponsor this tree-planting.

The Torah also recognises that people cannot continually take from the soil without enriching it. Jews were told that a piece of land must be left fallow every seventh year in order to maintain its productiveness.

Animals

In the Torah God said, '*I am putting you in charge of the fish, the birds, and all the wild animals*' (Genesis 1:28), which Jews interpret to mean that animals can be used by people as food or to work for them (see page 98 for more about the use of animals in medical experiments). There is much advice in the scriptures about the treatment of animals, all of which shows they should be treated with respect and consideration as part of God's creation. Even the fourth of the Ten Commandments stipulates that Shabbat must be a day of rest for animals as well as people: '*On that day no one is to work – neither you, your children, your slaves, your animals, nor the foreigners who live in your country.*' (Exodus 20:10) But that does not mean the animals should go hungry while the master rests; the Talmud is clear that a farmer must feed his animals first before he attends to his own needs.

Animals can be reared and killed for meat but this must be done with as much compassion as possible. Shechitah, the Jewish method of slaughter (see page 67), is believed to be as pain-free as possible because death is instantaneous. By contrast, hunting prolongs an animal's suffering and is forbidden. Animals may be used for medical experiments because this could save a human life, and the Torah says that the life of a person is of more value than an animal's.

What is...?

Tu B'Shevat is a spring festival in Israel when Jews plant trees to show their respect for God's creation.

Questions

  1 What Jewish festival shows concern for the environment?
  2 What is the Jewish attitude to animal rights, and why?
  3 Explain what is meant by people being God's stewards on earth.
  4 Do you think Jews would permit the use of animals for experiments relating to cosmetics? Give reasons for your answer.

Topic 2

Euthanasia

What is …?

Euthanasia is sometimes called 'mercy killing'. It means ending a person's life because they are in great pain or very old.

Euthanasia is the deliberate ending of a person's life. Euthanasia literally means 'to die well'. It is also known as 'mercy killing' because the intention is to end life in order to prevent a person suffering further. Death is carried out as quickly and painlessly as possible, enabling the person to die with dignity. This is illegal in Britain and in most countries, but some people believe that euthanasia should be allowed.

Voluntary euthanasia

This is a form of assisted suicide because the patients themselves ask for help in ending their life. It might be that a person has an incurable illness and asks for drugs which would kill them and prevent them suffering the rest of their life in pain.

Involuntary or compulsory euthanasia

Involuntary euthanasia is without the patient's consent. The decision may be taken to end the life of a seriously ill patient who is in a deep coma and not expected to recover. Many people believe in compulsory euthanasia

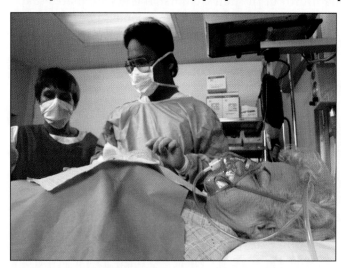

for an animal. If a pet dog is old or ill it can be 'put to sleep', but there is a debate about whether euthanasia is right for people. The danger is that some people may try to get rid of inconvenient relatives who are elderly, disabled or suffer from mental illness.

Jews permit life to be supported but not prolonged.

What do you think?

'Without your consent were you formed, without your consent were you born: without your consent you live and without your consent you will die.' What do you think this passage from the scriptures means? Does it give guidance to Jews on euthanasia?

Judaism and euthanasia

Jews look to the Torah for guidance on euthanasia, and it says many times that people were made by God and only God can decide when to end a life. Nobody is allowed to take another person's life.

> I am now giving you the choice between life and death, between God's blessing and God's curse, and I call heaven and earth to witness the choice you make. Choose life.
>
> (Deuteronomy 30:19)

> Then the Lord God took some soil from the ground and formed a man out of it; he breathed life-giving breath into his nostrils and the man began to live.
>
> (Genesis 2:7)

> If anyone takes human life, he will be punished.... Human beings were made like God, so whoever murders one of them will be killed by someone else.
>
> (Genesis 9:5–7)

> Do not commit murder.
>
> (Exodus 20:13 – this is the sixth of the Ten Commandments)

Jews are convinced that everyone has a part in God's plan and it is their duty to live and fulfil their role. Anyone who ends another's life is guilty of murder.

The technological advances of life-support machines have raised the question: at what point is life ended? The Talmud says: '*If there is anything which causes a hindrance to the departure of the soul ... then it is permissible to remove it.*' This has been interpreted to mean that if the vital organs have ceased functioning then a doctor should stop treatment. A life-support machine can be switched off, allowing God to decide when that life will end. It would be wrong to try to prolong a life that has ended. But there is a stark warning in the Talmud about hastening a person's death:

> He who closes the eyes of a dying man while the soul is still departing is shedding blood. This may be compared to a lamp that is going out; if a man places his finger upon it, it is immediately extinguished.

Doctors must support life and do everything in their power to save it but not try to prolong a life beyond its natural span.

❓ Questions

1 What does the word 'euthanasia' mean?
2 What does Judaism teach about euthanasia?
3 If a Jewish girl was in a coma after a car crash, should her parents allow her to be put on a life-support machine?

Topic 3 — Suffering

Free-will means that a person can make up their own mind how to act. They can choose to do good or evil. God does not intervene in that decision.

What do you think?

Can you think of any instance where good could come out of suffering?

Remember that the Lord your God corrects and punishes you just as a father disciplines his children.

(Deuteronomy 8:5)

Not to have known suffering is not to be truly human.

(Talmud)

God says: If I grant you happiness, give thanks; if I bring you suffering, give thanks.

(Talmud)

For Jews one of the hardest questions to answer is: 'Why does God let suffering happen?'

Jews believe God to be good, all-powerful and just, which makes it difficult to understand how God could cause suffering. If people were created in God's image as the Torah says, it seems hard to put the blame on them. Nevertheless the questions remain. Why do we suffer? How can God let this happen?

The collage of photographs on page 92 shows that the causes of suffering can be varied. Some are evidently inflicted by one person on another. Others we think of as natural disasters which nobody caused. Indeed they are commonly spoken of as 'acts of God'. Did God really make a flood or earthquake happen?

Over the centuries Jewish scholars have made detailed studies of the scriptures in their search for an understanding of suffering. Rabbi Moses Maimonides concluded that God creates humans with free-will and allows them to choose how to behave. If humans are to have free-will and a real choice between good and evil, both have to exist in the world. People who exercise their freedom to cause evil make people suffer. God cannot be blamed for people's cruelty. Suffering caused by famine, wars, pollution or poverty, it is claimed, is the result of human greed and cruelty, not God's actions.

> Man has been given free-will: if he wishes to turn toward the good way and to be righteous, the power is in his own hands; if he wishes to run toward the evil way and to be wicked, the power is likewise in his own hands.
>
> **Moses Maimonides**

How much of the suffering in the photographs do you think has been caused by people using their free-will to cause harm?

From study of the scriptures, rabbis found that suffering in the past usually served a purpose. It might be:

- a test of a person's faith in God, like the time when God asked Abraham to sacrifice his son Isaac
- a punishment for doing wrong which may teach someone a lesson and prevent them from making the same mistake again; for example, on occasions when the Jews disobeyed God's laws and worshipped statues they suffered defeat in battle and years of harsh rule by another power
- a way of making people repent for their wrong-doings and turn back to God
- a way to improve a person's character; for example, suffering could make someone patient or considerate towards others.

Jews believe that God only tests those who are strong enough to take it, and never more than they can endure. Although good can come out of suffering, it is still everyone's duty to try to relieve suffering whenever they can.

 **Questions**

1 What reasons do the Jewish scholars give for suffering?
2 How might a Jew explain why 6 million Jews were killed during the Holocaust?
3 'God should not be blamed when innocent people suffer.' Do you agree? Give reasons for your answer, showing that you have thought about more than one point of view.

Topic 4 Suicide

 What is ...?

If a person deliberately ends their own life it is called **suicide**. Jews believe this is a sin.

What do you think?

'A suicide should be pitied rather than condemned.' Do you agree? Would an Orthodox Jew agree with this statement?

Man Jumps Overboard

Jilted girl took overdose

Body found in car. Foul play not suspected.

In 73 CE a group of nearly 1,000 Jews were trapped on the top of this mountain fortress, with over 10,000 Roman soldiers besieging them. Rather than become slaves again, they destroyed all their property and committed suicide. Although this is totally forbidden under Jewish law, their action showed a determination to fight to defend their claim to the land of Israel and to choose death rather than slavery. But one woman and her children chose life, and survived to tell the story. Today soldiers in the Israeli Parachute Division swear an oath of allegiance at the top of Masada including the pledge that 'Masada shall not fall again!'

Suicide is the deliberate taking of your own life. Jews believe this is wrong. The Torah teaches: '*God created human beings, making them to be like himself.*' (Genesis 1:27) This means that humans were not responsible for their own beginning, so they have no right to end their life. Life is precious, and to destroy something made like God is a grave sin. Jews also believe it is their duty to live out the life God gave them so that they can take the part in creation which God intended for them.

The Torah states many times that if anyone takes a human life they will be punished because only God has the right to decide when that life is over.

> *I am now giving you the choice between life and death, between God's blessing and God's curse, and I call heaven and earth to witness the choice you make. Choose life.*
>
> **(Deuteronomy 30:19)**

> *I, and I alone, am God;*
> *no other god is real.*
> *I kill and I give life, I wound and I heal,*
> *and no one can oppose what I do.*
>
> **(Deuteronomy 32:39)**

> *The Lord gave, and now he has taken away. May his name be praised!*
>
> **(Job 1:21)**

> *Everything that happens in this world happens at the time God chooses. He sets the time for birth and the time for death.*
>
> **(Ecclesiastes 3:1–2)**

Jews know that there are some sad occasions when a person does take their own life. If it is likely they did it because they were worried, depressed, afraid or mentally unstable then this is not classed as suicide. Should a child commit suicide, it is not classed as suicide because children are not considered mature enough to understand the gravity of their action. Anyone who leaves evidence that they repented of their action at the last moment is forgiven.

If, however, a person committed suicide with a clear determination and was of sound mind, then Jews believe a terrible act has taken place. The person cannot be given the traditional funeral rites and their body must be buried in a separate part of the cemetery.

? Questions

1 Why do Jews regard suicide as a sin?
2 What is the Jewish teaching on suicide?
3 Under what circumstances could a Jew's suicide be forgiven?
4 Why do Jews regard the mass suicide of their people on Masada differently?

Topic 5

Contraception and abortion

> I am now giving you the choice between life and death, between God's blessing and God's curse, and I call heaven and earth to witness the choice you make. Choose life.
>
> (Deuteronomy 30:19)

This quotation from the Torah guides Jews in decisions about many life and death situations. How could it affect a Jewish woman's attitude towards abortion?

Judaism regards sex as a natural and healthy activity for married couples. Sex can be enjoyed for its own sake but also allows couples to share in God's work of creation by having children. The first command in the Torah is: '*Have many children, so that your descendants will live all over the earth.*' (Genesis 1:28) Because this is a mitzvah, or command, many Orthodox Jewish couples obey it and do not seek to limit the size of their family. Some Reform Jews believe the size of their family is their personal decision, while others think they should produce at least one son and daughter to fulfil the command.

Abortion

All Jews believe life is sacred and only God can choose when to end it. There is also general agreement in Judaism that life begins when a child is born, not when it is a foetus. The Halakhah, the Jewish Code of Law, does not approve of abortion but accepts that there may be times when an abortion is the right decision to protect the quality of an existing life. If a mother's physical health is endangered by the pregnancy, or if the birth of the child would cause her mental distress, then an abortion would be permitted. The life of a Jewish mother is always worth more than the potential life of her unborn child. Some Reform Jews would permit the abortion of a severely handicapped foetus if the mother requested it.

What is...?

Abortion is the deliberate removal and destruction of an unborn foetus. Judaism believes this is wrong unless the mother's life is at risk.

What do you think?

Do you think the rabbis would allow an abortion if a woman was raped? What issues are involved here?

Dear Leah,

I am expecting my second baby and I have just been for a scan. The doctor says it looks as though my baby will be severely handicapped. My husband and I are worried that we will never be able to cope with a badly handicapped child as well as our 2-year-old. Would I be allowed to have an abortion under Jewish Law?

Yours truly

Anne Goldsack

What advice would Leah, the Jewish Counsellor, give and why?

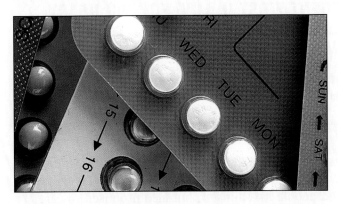

Judaism prefers the pill as a form of contraception because it allows sex to be as natural as possible.

Contraception

Orthodox Jews believe that babies are a gift from God, allowing people to have their part to play in God's plan for the world. They do not approve of contraception unless the mother's health is at risk from a pregnancy. Reform Jews think it is acceptable to use contraception to limit the size of their family. All Jews are agreed that contraception is preferable to abortion.

The Halakhah says that sex should be as natural as possible. The rabbis have decided that if contraception is to be used, the pill is preferable to the condom because sex should be as natural as possible, and the commands in the Torah to have children were directed to the man. Orthodox Jews do not permit a vasectomy because it is regarded as mutilation of the body. Reform Jews believe methods of contraception are a personal choice.

Questions

1 What is **a** abortion and **b** contraception?
2 What does Judaism teach about abortion?
3 What is the Orthodox attitude towards contraception?
4 Why do Orthodox Jews think it is important to have a large family?

Medical ethics

What do you think?

> **JEWISH PATIENT FIRST IN LINE FOR PIG HEART**
>
> *Sunday Times, 12 May 1998*
>
> What sort of issues does this raise? Do you think a Jew would accept a pig's heart?

'*I, the Lord, am your healer.*' (Exodus 15:26) This passage from the Torah underpins the whole Jewish attitude towards medical ethics. Jews believe that God not only created people like himself, but also promised to care for them. This belief is repeated every day in the morning prayer when God is described as '*the healer of all flesh*'. It is by using the skill of doctors that Jews believe God heals sick people.

Judaism is called 'a life-affirming religion', which means saving life is one of the most important considerations. When it comes to decisions about abortion, the existing life of the mother takes priority over her unborn child.

The use of drugs to relieve pain is acceptable to Jews but their use for recreation is totally banned. The great rabbi Maimonides said:

> *Keeping the body fit and healthy is part of serving God, for it is impossible to know or understand anything of the Creator's will if one is ill. Therefore a person should avoid whatever undermines bodily health.*

Medical experiments

Jews believe that it is correct to try out new methods of treatment in order to save lives. If this involves medical experiments on animals then it is permitted. Whilst animals are also part of God's creation, they are considered lower than humans. When animals are used for medical experiments they must be treated as humanely as possible and not made to suffer unnecessarily. Jews believe that people can volunteer to take part in clinical trials of a new drug or treatment before it goes into general use provided there is no serious risk to their own health.

Organ transplants

Jews believe that God made humans and therefore a person's body is not their property to abuse. Organ donation is permitted, however, if it will save the life of another and nobody's life is put at risk. However, no one can end a life prematurely in order to obtain a fresh organ for transplant. Look back to page 91 to understand the Jewish attitude to life-support machines.

Fertility treatment

Jews believe that having a family is of great importance. This means that Jewish doctors can assist a woman to have children. In the Torah, God intervened to give Sarah, the elderly wife of Abraham, a child after she had tried for many years to have a baby. Artificial insemination is acceptable, provided that the sperm used is the husband's. Sperm from anyone else, even an anonymous donor, is forbidden as a form of adultery. The same ruling means that a woman can have a fertilised egg implanted in her womb if the egg was hers. *In vitro* fertilisation, producing what is popularly called 'a test-tube baby', is also allowed provided the embryos are looked after with the respect due to a potential human life. Surrogacy, where a woman has a baby for another woman, is considered a misuse of a human body and so is forbidden.

Jewish doctors are permitted to carry out research on human embryos provided the embryos were not bred specifically for experiments. Even embryos are God's creation and must be handled and disposed of with respect.

Post-mortems are regarded as a mutilation of the human body, but, if the coroner requires it by law, it must be carried out. Jews also accept that a post-mortem may assist in saving a future life and so should be permitted.

This is Lord Winston, a famous Jewish doctor who specialises in treating couples who cannot have children.

? Questions

1 How do Jews think God heals people?
2 Can Jewish women receive fertility treatment?
3 'Animals are less important than people.' Do you agree? Give reasons for your answer, showing that you have thought about the Jewish attitude towards the use of animals in experiments.
4 What religious considerations are involved in a Jew donating their body for medical research?

Do you understand...

Jewish attitudes to life and death?

Task 1

1 Why do Jews not agree with euthanasia?
2 'Against your will you must live.' (Ethics of the Fathers) What implications does this teaching of the rabbis have for the Jewish teaching about suicide?
3 How would a Jewish doctor decide whether a terminally ill patient should remain on a life-support machine?

Task 2

1 What is the Jewish attitude towards hunting?
2 Can a Jew kill an animal for food, or must they be vegetarian?
3 'Animals have as much right to life as us.' Do you agree? Explain the reasons for your answer, taking care to consider how an Orthodox Jew might respond.

Task 3

1 What good do Jews think could come from suffering?
2 'If God really loved humanity we would never have to suffer.' Do you
   agree? Give reasons to support your answer, and show that you have
   thought about different points of view.

Task 4

*'You appointed them rulers over everything you made; you placed them over all
creation: sheep and cattle, and the wild animals too; the birds and the fish and
the creatures in the seas.'* (Psalms 8:6–8)

1 What do Jews mean when they say 'humans are stewards on the earth'?
2 What implications does the quotation above have for the position of
   animals on earth?
3 Give a practical example of the way in which Jews should care for the
   planet.

Task 5

How many of these terms can you define?
• involuntary euthanasia   • suicide   • abortion
• stewardship   • contraception

✓ Quick revision

• God created the world, so people must respect it.
• Humans are stewards not owners of the world.
• Humans not God cause suffering.
• Only God gives life and only God can take it away.
• A human life is worth more than an animal's.

Revision

Checklist

Before you begin your revision, you need to check the following points with your teacher.

- You need to know which examination board's syllabus you have studied.
- You need to know how the syllabus expects you to use the information and knowledge you have studied in this book.
- You need to know which biblical passages the examination board expects you to have studied in detail.
- You need to know the format of the examination paper. Will you have to answer all questions, or will there be a choice? Will there be different types of questions, ranging from short answers to essays?
- You need to know the date, time and length of the examination paper.

Preparation

Once you have all this information from your teacher, you need to organise your notes. Make sure that you have covered all the topics in the syllabus. If you have any information missing, make sure that you copy up the work.

Revision timetable

Organise your revision time carefully. It is never too early to start revision. Work out how many weeks are left before your 'mock' examination or the GCSE examinations start. Make a plan of all the topics you need to revise and all the leisure activities you wish to continue during the revision period. Fill in study periods and leisure periods. At the beginning of each week decide which topics you are going to study during that week.

Allow some flexibility in your timetable, as you do not know what unexpected events may happen. **Do not leave revision until the last minute.**

Make the best use of your revision time.

- You need a suitable environment in which to revise. Some people like to revise in total silence, while others prefer music in the background. Use whichever method helps your revision.
- You need to get down to work according to the timetable that *you* have drawn up. Revise the topic you have planned to do and have written down.
- Sitting staring at a page or set of notes is not the best use of revision time.

Acknowledgements
With thanks to the following for permission to reproduce photographs and other copyright material in this book:

Steve Allen Photography: 7
Andes Press Agency: Carlos Reyes-Manzo 9, 20, 29, 30, 34 (bottom), 53, 68, 78 (right)
ASAP: 36, 40 (bottom), 52 (top), 54, 56 (right), 62
Associated Press: 82, 86 (top), 92 (all except top right), 100
Circa Photolibrary: Barry Searle 19, 24, 48, 52 (bottom), Jed Murray 65
Sonia Halliday Photographs: David Silverman 12 (top), 15, Bryan Knox 34 (top), 40 (top), 50
Hodder & Stoughton: 70
Alex Keene/ The Walking Camera: 38, 78 (left)
KKL-JNF Photo Archive: 88
Manchester Jewish Museum: 16 (both)
Press Association: 75, 99
Rex Features: 76
Science Photo Library: 97
Martin Sookias: 44, 63
Ina Taylor: 10, 11, 12 (bottom), 14, 58, 60, 61, 64, 66, 72, 85, 87, 94
Tzedek: 81, 86 (bottom)
Wiener Library: 84, 92 (top right), 101
Jerry Wooldridge: 26, 32, 42, 56 (left)

Every effort has been made to contact copyright holders. The publishers apologise to anyone whose rights have been inadvertently overlooked, and will be happy to rectify any errors or omissions.

Revision techniques

Successful revision involves active learning. There are a variety of revision techniques that can help you to understand and memorise information. You need to find which technique is best for you.

Note-taking
- Summaries of your work can help you remember the information. As you study each section of your notes, write down the important points.
- Learn these points and then cover up the notes and rewrite them from memory.
- Check off your list from memory against your original list, and note any points you got wrong or forgot to include.

Practise past questions
- Use past questions that you have worked through in class, or questions from past examination papers, to help you understand the work.
- Answer the questions, in note form, using your notes.
- Cover up your answer and work through the question again without notes.
- Check off your answer from memory against your original list, and note any points you got wrong or forgot to include.

Use the 'Do you understand' sections of this book
Work through each set of tasks in each of the sections in this book to help you to develop your skills and understanding.

Ask relatives and friends to test you
Give them your notes and ask them to test you on the information. Make sure that they tell you the right answer, if you get questions wrong.

Final preparation
- Make sure that you have a good night's sleep before the examination.
- Take several pens and pencils into the examination room.
- Read the examination questions carefully and do not rush your answers.
- If you have time at the end of the examination, check through your answers.